ADVANCE PRAISE FOR

"As an avid reader, I couldn't put this book down. It's one of those rare cover-to-cover reads that tells His story —that is, God's story —through his story (that is, Scott's story). Scott's smile on the book's cover tells it all. *To God be the glory, great things He has done.*"

—Larry Rea, Memphis *Commercial Appeal* sportswriter
and host of the *Outdoors with Larry Rea* radio show

"I want to especially thank you for the gentle, caring way you share your story. God has taught you so much over the years, but it is obvious that your wheelchair isn't a 'bully pulpit,' but a platform that showcases grace and humility. God bless you for showing us what's best about being broken. Hebrews 6:10 says, 'For God is not unjust: he will not forget your work and the love you have shown him as you have helped his people and continue to help them.' I always say, people's stories will not change lives, but a personal testimony infused with Scripture will."

—Joni Eareckson Tada, Joni and Friends
International Disability Center

"Nothing can supplant a life well lived. The only day that is important is today. God bless all the Coleman family for being such a good example, for enduring and confronting adversity with such faith, purpose, determination, and cheer! 'But the greatest of these is love!' And your love is abundantly evident."

—Bob Byrd, Chairman of the Board
and CEO Bank of Bartlett, Tennessee

"… Your attitude and your family's attitude awe me. Since reading your book, I am much more cheerful and taking things as they come with more hope. Thank you for brightening my day!"

—Gertie Tribo of Cordova, Tennessee

"I hope Linda told you how much I enjoyed your book. Not sure if I laughed or cried harder! It ended leaving me wanting more ... Are you up for the sequel?"

— Peggy Lovell of Memphis, Tennessee

"I thought before I read it, *It will be interesting to read what Scott went through because it is so unlike anything I have known.* That turned out to be untrue. I love the title. I really love the title. I have learned this very thing in the last thirty years as well. Sara is best when broken. The problem is I keep rebuilding the old self and then I go through the pain all over again. C. S. Lewis in *Mere Christianity* sums it up: 'I must be plowed up and resown.' Your book is Christ centered and focused on Him. Your book is all about what God did in you, through and because of Christ. I believe it will send others to Him. It is a complete joy to listen to a fellow sojourner's story of grace! It reminds me of the grace shown to me. It causes me to stop and praise Him."

—Sara Harbuck Doyle of Denver, Colorado

"You are a testimony in faith and perseverance, but you shared so much more in your story. You told how important relationships are and how others have helped you become the man you are today. You reminded us to go, do, or move when the Holy Spirit tells us because we never know what impact we might be having on another person's life. As a parent of twenty-two and twenty-four-year-old daughters, it is encouraging to know that parents' love, wisdom, and care go a long way in their children's lives. You also reminded me to cherish each moment and be thankful for the blessings I have today. I am thankful you chose to let us in on the stories that shaped you."

—Tina Ross Holland of Tupelo, Mississippi

"Beth Moore says, '...Have the courage to live a life under strain and pain to be part of the better story. A larger story. Don't wimp out.' You are the poster person for this quote, especially since you started writing your book. You have made a huge impact on many lives. Thank you for not 'wimping out.' You are a true blessing from our Father."

—Melissa Gibbs of Collierville, Tennessee

"Psalm 46:10: '... be still and know that I am God.' As I read the book Best When Broken, one point that impacted my life was Scott's inability to hurry through life as most of us do. His accident **forced** him to slow his pace. Actually, for a while it virtually caused him to stop living as most of us know it. What began as a tragedy became a blessing, as Scott is now able to 'be still' and truly appreciate all that God has created in His beautiful world."

—Pam Fields, International Paper Human Resources

"What a great testimony. After many years of doing business with you, I know your heart and your love for our God. You came into my life thirteen years ago when I seriously needed answers with a son-in-law paralyzed from the neck down in a car accident. You'll never know what your words of love and hope meant to me. Since then I have a son paralyzed from the waist down and a wife that has to have twenty-four-hour care after suffering a fifteen-foot fall. I read your book in one day and was so moved by it I had a special time with my God that day. What a great blessing and inspiration you are to all who come in contact and do business with you every day. God is using you in a special way, and you are in my prayers always. Thanks for being you."

—Wayne Gaunce, Gaunce Management

"Scott's journey did not end the day of the accident. Scott found that he was at his best when he was broken. The story exposes the reality of being broken. It is not pretty. But it also exposes the beauty of being broken. For Scott, life did not end that day but really began. I encourage the readers to join the journey and find how your brokenness makes you better. Your brokenness becomes the canvas upon which God paints His masterpiece. Your brokenness gives others a chance to find their joy. You will laugh. You'll cry. You may even pull a muscle. But one thing for sure, you'll enjoy the journey through Scott's story."

—Clayton Cloer, PhD, Senior Pastor of
First Baptist Church of Central Florida

BEST WHEN BROKEN

Even the young grow weary and tired,
and young men stumble and fall.

Scott Coleman

WESTBOW
PRESS
A DIVISION OF THOMAS NELSON

WestBow Press books may be ordered through booksellers or by contacting:

WestBow Press
A Division of Thomas Nelson
1663 Liberty Drive
Bloomington, IN 47403
www.westbowpress.com
1-(866) 928-1240

Because of the dynamic nature of the Internet, any web addresses or links contained in this book may have changed since publication and may no longer be valid. The views expressed in this work are solely those of the author and do not necessarily reflect the views of the publisher, and the publisher hereby disclaims any responsibility for them.

Any people depicted in stock imagery provided by Thinkstock are models, and such images are being used for illustrative purposes only.

Certain stock imagery © Thinkstock.

ISBN: 978-1-4497-5871-4 (sc)
ISBN: 978-1-4497-5872-1 (hc)
ISBN: 978-1-4497-5870-7 (e)

Library of Congress Control Number: 2012912375

Printed in the United States of America

WestBow Press rev. date: 10/02/2012

CONTENTS

"Broken Ain't Bad!" ix

Dedication xiii

One more "Thank You"! xv

Isaiah 40:28–31 xvii

Introduction by Wes Hoggard xix

Is There Anything More Wonderful Than Grace? 1

This Is Long Overdue … and If I Don't Put
     It on Paper, I Might Burst! 2

Next Stop, Eternity! 5

Life Was Dang Near Perfect .7

Back to the Bottom of the Lake 17

One Flew over the Cuckoo's Nest 20

Reality Sinks in, and the Battle Begins! 26

It's Not Your Battle! 43

The Power in "Ditch Digging" 49

A Body in Motion 56

I Was Missing So Much and Sure I Would Have
     Missed Even More! 63

Getting Back to the Wilderness 65

Abundant Joyful Adventure 80
Travel Pictures 83
Slow Enough to Notice 86
Shirley Temple Was Naïve or the Upside of
      Reaching the End of Me 91
Epilogue 95
Afterword 100
Pictures from Today 123

"BROKEN AIN'T BAD!"

I'm quick to pop off at the mouth encouraging everyone to frequently "take inventory" of themselves and I "think" that I make a conscious decision to do this on a regular basis. But my heart is so wicked and impossible for me to know. Inventory is impossible to take by yourself.

But it has been a long time since I took a very very hard look at my life. I thought a part of my motivation... Or at least I'd hoped my motivation was pure when it came to the book. Glorify God. Point people away from me and finally express that I truly am filthy rags if it were not for God and the wonderful friends who really, really, really know me and everything that comes with me... And they love me anyway.

I revisited about 10 different articles that even went back to high school. I did not recognize myself in any of them. Yet without exception, my initial response has always been pride...... but I have this Person living inside of me. This Person stirs my spirit even when I think I know exactly who I am... And when I finally get over my pride I feel embarrassing humiliation that the article painted a picture of me that is so flattering it makes me sick at my stomach. It has triggered depression on more than one occasion.

The only one I can laugh about now is the article that said I was drafted by the major leagues to play baseball when I was in high school… I wasn't very good at baseball and when Linda and I read it we laughed for about a split second and then we wanted to crawl under a rock.

While trying to write I frequently have been crying and I've not been able to really figure out why. Poor Linda. But I think it all came together for me in the way it always has.

Selfish pride and enjoying attention came on my radar through circumstances, conversation and contemplation. Then I started reading the Bible.

One night I read dozens of chapters in Psalms that were written by David. If you did not know the man you would wonder if he was a flake, manic depressive, or having a mental breakdown. His highs were incredibly high, and his lows were devastating.

If people are going to write a song about you like "Saul has killed his thousands, but David has killed his 10,000s", you better surround yourself with friends like Nathan who pointed his finger at King David and said "U DA MAN!"

I kept reading, praying and trying to figure out how it all made sense?

Eureka! I honestly believe that you never get to experience the full joy of your salvation until you come to a proper understanding of filthy rags and who you really are. The irony of the Christian life is sometimes… well, most of the time if not always the journey on the way to joy sometimes begins with a visit to the dung heap that is me. And then when I consider how much God loves me to do what he did for me in all my worthlessness…

A discerning friend who always has time to listen and asked so many wonderful questions called one morning. Sometime in the conversation I said to him what I have said to him many times before… "How do you write a story about your life that is not about you"? He understood exactly what I meant.

So as I was thinking and praying and trying to figure out what was going on inside of me I realized that God says in his word, "You can do nothing apart from Me". But what does "nothing" mean......Hmmmm? Well, "nothing" means by golly nothing! So I have been "trying" with all of my own effort, creativity, strength, cleverness and it just occurred to me that exactly what I'm trying to communicate in the book is... I do not have what it takes and have never had what it takes...

When I get out of God's way... Focus on him... Take inventory and realize I am nothing... I become broken...

When this happens God gives me purpose, power, passion, productivity and overwhelming joy.

I am definitely "BEST WHEN BROKEN."

DEDICATION

There is a passage in the Bible that says that sometimes we are in the presence of angels but unaware. I could easily dedicate this book to the countless strangers who open doors for me, help me or Linda with things I've dropped, help me recover from an embarrassing moment, or simply smile and give me a word of encouragement.

But there are also a significant amount of people in my life who are literally gifts from God, beginning with Linda, my parents, and my sister, Kelly. Mom and Dad were encouraged from day one to find "professional" help to take care of me on a daily basis either in a separate facility or at home. They never even considered it, and I seriously doubt I would be alive if they would've taken that option. Kelly immediately left the college she was attending so she could simply come home, be my friend, love me, and take care of me. To this day, Kelly and her family are some of my closest friends and make me smile just thinking about them. My nieces and nephews are dear to me.

It's not even possible to put into words what my wife, Linda, has done for me and what she means to me. She is my best friend. I joke sometimes that I am living this life because I was and am a klutz. Linda knew everything she was giving up by marrying me. She knew that life was not going to be easy, and forget about the "unknowns." The "knowns" are more than enough to scare even most friends away. She knew all this from the beginning, chose to love me, and lived this life that no one would volunteer for. Her love and sacrifice overwhelm me.

There are at least a dozen friends I could dedicate this book to, and I will mention quite a few of them in the following pages; however, there is one friend who is the poster child of what a friend should be, and that's Wes Hoggard. First, I probably would not have finished this book without his encouragement. Secondly, he has been a role model to me in so many ways but particularly when it comes to taking the road less traveled. Wes and a few others always seem to be "right on time," always there when I need them.

So this is for all of the above, the strangers, my family, my friends, my wonderful Sunday school class, and especially all of those children who climb all over me and call me "Skwat."

My girl!

One more "Thank You"!

It's never been my battle!

I was clueless about how difficult writing this story would be. At times spiritually, emotionally and physically brutal all at once.

Just like everything in my life I'd be hopeless if not for caring friends.

Writing is lonely work and on some days a simple "how are you doing?" kept me going.

I've needed frequent help for some pretty simple tasks that are impossible for me, or might take me a week when an able body person could do the same in an hour.

Turning pages in a picture album. Navigating through picture files. Correcting excessive punctuation errors. Repeatedly reading every draft. All tedious and boring.

I can't remember a day when Linda wasn't doing something to help or serve someone, so I've tried to spare her all of this drudgery.

Friends have repeatedly stepped up and I'm grateful.

The Lord and the friends He's blessed me with have always fought my battles.

Just like Jehosaphat in the twentieth chapter of Second Chronicles, my battles are frequently fought by others.

I would be very pleased if I knew my tombstone would simply read, "He was grateful!"

Scott

March 10, 2012

Isaiah 40:28-31

Do you not know?
Have you not heard?

The Lord is everlasting God,
the Creator of the ends of the earth.

He will not grow tired or weary,
and his understanding no one can fathom.

He gives strength to the weary
increases the power of the weak.

Even youths grow tired and weary,
and young men stumble and fall;

But those who hope in the Lord
will renew their strength.

They will soar on wings like eagles;
they will run and not grow weary;
they will walk and not be faint.

INTRODUCTION BY WES HOGGARD

In 1978, William Scott Coleman and I attended the same private high school in Memphis, Tennessee. As a senior playing high school sports, I knew that Scott, who was a freshman at the time, was a very talented athlete. He was the starting quarterback for the freshman football team and excelled in basketball, track, and any other sports he participated in. Scott was chosen as Mr. Freshman his ninth-grade year. Scott was a large boy for his age. He had blond hair and was already breaking girls' hearts at an early age. I remember one evening when I went to his house. He came to greet me at the door in brown gym shorts, and he was playing a twelve-string guitar. He was playing and singing "Stairway to Heaven." To this day, I still remember thinking, *Is there anything this kid can't do?* I was convinced that one day I would be watching him on Saturday afternoons, playing football for his favorite college, the Auburn Tigers. Little did I know how much this young man would influence not only my life but also the lives of many others in the coming years, including my future wife and children. On June 22, 1980, at the age of seventeen, Scott was involved in a tragic waterskiing accident that ended his dreams of playing sports and altered his life and the lives of many others close to him.

This is a story of his parents' expectations, and not excuses, a young man who refused to quit, and a family that stood by him even under the harshest conditions. As a parent of three children, I cannot begin to imagine the heartache, tension, anxiety, and helplessness that his parents and sister must have suffered during the first days and months after Scott's tragic ordeal. In a society that seems to always have something to complain about, after thirty years since his accident, I have never seen, heard, or even felt like any one of them have ever had a pity party, at least not out in public.

How does one at such a young age deal with a severely crippling accident, finish high school, graduate from college, get married, and land a great job to financially support him and his wife? Scott recently built Linda and himself a beautiful getaway cabin. Scott and Linda did all this without any government help, and the Coleman family never sued anyone over his accident.

For those who don't believe there are angels on earth, they have never met his wife, Linda. Why would a young, attractive, smart girl marry a man confined in a wheelchair with little money, knowing that she would have to give up so much of what we take for granted to care for him for the rest of her life? Her love for Scott reaches bounds that the average person's imagination cannot comprehend. A friend of mine made a comment that he knew when he got to heaven she would have a seat reserved in the VIP section, and I couldn't agree more.

I struggle to find the words to describe what Scott and his family have meant to me over the years. Many times when I think I have troubles, he comes to mind. I realize that my problems are miniscule compared to what he endures every day. This is not a sad story but a story of triumph and what unconditional love, commitment, faith in God, and the human spirit can endure and overcome when all these elements are combined. My family and I have been truly blessed to have been a small part of his life. It seems the older I get, the harder it is for me to find a hero—that is, until I think of Scott and his family. I am sure you will agree.

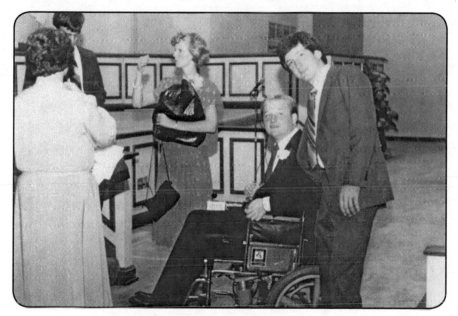

Wedding Rehearsal with Wes

Is There Anything More Wonderful Than Grace?

"They" said I probably wouldn't live. If I survived, they recommended my parents find an institution that could take care of me. "They" said I would need to seek assistance from the government, because an unemployable quadriplegic would need to get a government check just to cover ongoing medical needs. In recent years, Mom, who loves me more than anyone, has told me she prayed that God would not let me live if my life would be as "they" predicted. Wow!

Six years later, I graduated from high school and college and was hired as a stockbroker trainee. In 1986, when Linda and I got married, we had no money. I was dialing the phone with my tongue and writing with a pen in my mouth. I was on full commission and had zero clients. I would not have hired me, and I certainly would not have married me! But I wasn't in a nursing home; I was married to my best friend and having more fun than just about anybody I knew.

THIS IS LONG OVERDUE ... AND IF I DON'T PUT IT ON PAPER, I MIGHT BURST!

I would not believe it myself. It could have been a horror story. Instead of *It's a Wonderful Life,* my story could easily be *What a Waste.* If you had told me exactly what was going to happen to me physically, I think I would've said, "Shoot me now!" If you knew me like I know me, you probably would've volunteered to buy the bullets. I underestimated my family. I underestimated my friends. I underestimated my God. I am eternally grateful. I could live one thousand lifetimes and never express the gratitude for the family and friends God has given me.

It embarrasses me to admit how many moments I've wasted worrying about things that never came to pass—moments that should have been productive and joyful wasted because I was emotionally in the fetal position. I constantly battle the urge to make a knowingly stupid decision that would train-wreck every one of the blessings in my life. A major part of the reason for my attempt to put this on paper is to remind myself of how blessed I truly am and revisit the times in my life when my faith supplied me with peace and joy beyond comprehension in spite of circumstances. I also hope someone may be encouraged by what I write. Life is absolutely wonderful when our focus is on the right things.

I also wanted to finally set the record straight before too much time went by. Many wonderful people have written flattering articles about me, but I've never really been satisfied that they hit the mark. Some have exaggerated to the point that I was horribly embarrassed. It feels so good to be praised! Even when I know I'm getting undeserved credit, I endorse their assessment by simply smiling and saying, "Aw, shucks!"

I am a big fan of grace. I am grateful for grace. *Grace* is when someone knows you intimately, not physically, and knows your heart, your fears, your dreams, what embarrasses you, and how you are at your worst but loves you anyway.

Anything that is attractive in my life is the result of the wonderful grace of God. I have frequently taken credit when I have deserved none. There have been many times in my life that a close observer would have no idea that I am a Christian. How can an average guy who can't control or feel 95 percent of his body be happy? Have fun? Be joyful? Sometimes even I can't fully explain it, but I thought it was long overdue to at least attempt to put it on paper.

I also need to thank all of you who really know me and love me anyway! Without all of you, I really would have simply quit. Gratitude compels me to write and gives me the energy and enthusiasm to go to work every day. I cannot count the times in the last twenty-eight years that I have reached the end of Scott, pity parties in every area of my life, exhausted, defeated, humiliated, discouraged, and wanting to curl up in the fetal position and fulfill the original prophecy "they" had for my life. Stinking it up comes so easily for me. I have firsthand knowledge of what Luther meant when he confessed to being a "snow-covered dung heap." I am amazed at how vicious my speech can be. You would think someone who had to control only four or five muscles in his body could certainly control his tongue. Well, not me!

I believe God provided me with willing encouragers at every point of crisis. Family, friends, clients, and strangers have always provided exactly what I needed when I needed it to make it one more day. This rotating group of encouragers not only kept me going but also transformed my train wreck into a wonderfully abundant life.

It has occurred to me that one day it really will be too late to say thank you. It seems like in a blink of an eye, Pepaw is gone. Memaw is gone. Granddaddy is gone. Grandmother is gone. Jere is gone. Corky is gone. Owen is gone. Jimmy is gone. Bill is gone. Monty is gone. Norm is gone. Many others are gone too. I know in a blink of an eye, I will be gone. If I leave before I share some things, I will have left some things undone.

I hope I can come close to expressing my gratitude.

NEXT STOP, ETERNITY!

Just a few minutes before my accident.

If you were sure you were going to die in the next few moments and undoubtedly headed straight to eternity, what might you be thinking? Take a moment and remember who you were at age 17. Do your best to think what might be on your mind if you found yourself in the following situation. You are facedown in Sardis Lake at Les Pedeza Point Mississippi. You have just taken an unexpected deep dive from water skis in very shallow water. You have shredded your spinal cord. You cannot move a muscle and you obviously cannot breathe. Other than the pain of busting your nose, it really doesn't hurt. The explosion of noise you hear at impact is almost unbearable. Your cervical fourth and fifth vertebrae have just been shattered into little pieces. Upon impact the noise reminds you of the sensation you have while sitting in a great theater with surround sound. . You literally feel the noise in every part of your body. It is very similar to the noise that accompanies an avalanche or a high-rise being demolished. To say you are numb or have lost all sensation is not accurate. The sensation is horrifically frightening and is very similar to the way a body part feels when you have been sitting in an awkward position and the blood flow has stopped. My sister Kelly and I used to say that our leg or foot had "fallen asleep" or "resigned." It feels as if an electric current is running through your entire body. It will frequently feel like this for the rest of your life.

Please put this book down for just a minute and give serious consideration to what you are thinking.

Life Was Dang Near Perfect

But what am I thinking? Let me take a little detour and try to describe briefly my life growing up before the accident. This will let you get inside my head on that particular day and at that particular moment.

My dad loves to tell stories about when he was growing up. Inevitably, before the story is over, he will comment about what a wonderful time the '50s were to live in and to be in high school. Maybe everyone feels this way. I know some people aren't so fortunate, but if anyone had better parents, a better sister, better grandparents, better friends, and more fun than I had, I have not met him.

We moved from Birmingham, Alabama, to Memphis, Tennessee, when I was in first grade. Dad had been transferred with his company, and we left the city where my parents had grown up and where my grandparents and other relatives still lived.

I think my sister would probably agree that the most wonderful thing Mom and Dad did for both of us was make us a priority. Even from an early age, we knew every decision they made began and ended with how my sister and I would be affected. Being someone's priority is an incredible gift. When you are confident you are loved that much, it compels you to always consider those who love you when you are faced with a tough decision. This alone kept me out of a significant amount of trouble. It also gave me confidence in almost every setting and every crowd.

All of my grandparents have been in heaven for quite a few years, but the dominant memory I have of all of them is how much they loved us. Both of my grandmothers were stay-at-home moms, and my dad's dad was a city detective in Birmingham for forty years. My "Pepaw" was the business manager of a Mack truck dealership.

Granddaddy Coleman had me in the woods, hunting and fishing from a very early age, and Pepaw Young helped me develop a love for college football at a very young age, especially Auburn football! Pepaw also subscribed to *Forbes* magazine, and I can remember as a teenager being fascinated by what I was reading but comprehending very little of it.

Daddy was a regional sales manager for a pharmaceutical company and was out one or two nights a week. Mother was at home, taking care of "mother stuff."

The quickest way for me to get my fanny whipped was for Dad to come home and find I'd not watered and fed our hunting dogs and cleaned their pens. Kelly and I always had chores that had to be completed if we wanted to receive our weekly allowances. Most of mine involved the yard or the dog pen. As I got older, my responsibilities increased. Beginning when I was about twelve or thirteen, I was expected to earn my spending money by mowing yards. And by the time I could drive, I was expected to have a summer job, which always ended up being construction work for a company one of our friends owned.

Our neighborhood was family-friendly and safe for even the youngest children to play outside all day long without moms and dads being concerned about much more than someone getting a black eye or skinned knees. It was definitely a different day, and on a regular basis, a baseball game or hide-and-seek might quickly deteriorate into a fistfight.

Fighting was simply the result of young boys being competitive, and most of the time, it ended with a shaking of hands, a fat lip, and a lesson learned. My dad is one of the most tender-hearted persons on the planet, but beginning in third grade when he caught wind that I was being bullied a little bit at school, he explained to me in no uncertain terms what he expected. I was never to start a fight or bully anyone, but I was also never to back away, especially if a bully was picking on me or a friend.

To this day, I am grateful that Daddy taught me how to hold my ground and take care of myself. I obviously haven't been in a fistfight since I was a teenager, but on a regular basis, there's something in life that requires the same kind of effort.

Mom was not always enthusiastic about his encouragement. Three different stories illustrate almost perfectly what seemed to happen on a regular basis in our neighborhood.

The first time I can ever remember even wrestling with another boy was in third grade. There were twin brothers who were the meanest kids in the neighborhood. Every day during recess, they would terrorize my friends and me by kicking, tackling, or punching one of us. I can remember my biggest fear was not that they would hurt me but that I would get in trouble and disappoint Mom and Dad. When Dad found out, he was more disappointed that I was continuing to let it happen and explained the facts of life to me. I was not to let this ever happen again, and if I got in trouble defending myself or a friend, he would pick me up from school and immediately take me to get a milkshake! That's all I needed to hear. One afternoon as I was walking out of the YMCA (Young Men's Christian Association) after a basketball practice, one of the "brothers" kicked me in the rump when my back was turned. I'm not sure of everything that happened in the next few moments, but all of a sudden, two of the brothers were lying on the ground and crying, and I was steadily punching both of them with all of my strength. I think I was actually enjoying myself until I looked up and there was Mom giving me "that look". When Mom gave you that particular look, you knew beyond a shadow of a doubt that you were in deep trouble. She simply turned around and started walking, with me following at a cautious distance. As we were headed home, she asked me one question: "Scott, do you know what YMCA stands for?" That was all she needed to say. Dad bought me a milkshake!

Several years later, I had been avoiding an older, very big boy in our neighborhood named Herman. I really can't remember what I had done that angered him so much, but word on the street was that Herman was going to put something on me that soap could not remove. I would either stay inside when I knew he was in the neighborhood or walk a mile out of the way to avoid an ugly encounter. He was a big boy.

I was helping Dad, or in hindsight, I was probably complaining to him about the yard work that he was making me do on a beautiful summer afternoon. I looked up and saw Herman walking our way. I didn't panic at all because what boy in his right mind would come give you a beating in your own front yard with your dad standing there? Herman obviously didn't think that way. He walked straight up to Dad and said, "Mr. Coleman, would you mind if I fought Scott?"

I thought this boy was an idiot and was totally amused until Dad looked at me and simply said, "Put your rake down, son."

What the—

The back of my head literally hit the ground before my rake did! He beat the tar out of me for several minutes, and when finished, he shook Dad's hand and said, "Thank you very much, Mr. Coleman."

I thought that at least I would not have to do yard work anymore. Once again, I was clueless. Dad looked at me with a grin on his face and said, "Scott, stand up and get back to work." The only other comment was that he had told me my entire life that when I knew it was inevitable that I should never let someone strike the first blow. . That was the last fight I ever lost.

One other story completes the whole picture. My sophomore year, Dad came to pick me up after a football practice. When I got in the car, he told me what was going to greet me when I got home. Once again, there was a very big, very bold bully in the neighborhood I had upset. I thought I was a pretty nice guy, but for some reason, I was a bully magnet. This boy had knocked on our front door and asked Dad if I could come outside, because he intended to give me a beating. According to Mom, Dad enthusiastically said, "If you will wait here for about twenty minutes, I am sure Scott will be happy to accommodate you when I bring him home from football practice." Unbelievable. Remember, it was a different day.

The entire way home, Dad reminded me that whatever I did, this encounter was inevitable and I'd better not let him get the first lick on me. By the time we pulled into the driveway, word had spread, and our front yard probably had twenty-five or thirty children anxiously anticipating this entertainment.

I struck the first blow that day, and once again, I learned that life was so much easier when I listened to Dad. Mom just gave me "the look."

Why do I even mention these stories? I am grateful to Mom and Dad for teaching me a work ethic and teaching me that in life, someone or something is occasionally going to require a battle.

We were Baptist to the bone. Both of my grandparents were Baptist. Even when I was in the womb, we attended a Baptist church almost every time the doors were open. Mom and Dad never preached to me or Kelly. But from a very early age, I was taught that all of us had fallen short of what was required to have a relationship with the one true, holy God, but wonderfully through an act of grace, Jesus had provided a way to restore the relationship. It was impossible to be "good enough" to get to heaven, but that was not what God required. He required repentance and faith in what was accomplished on the cross.

On our street alone, we had Catholic friends, Methodist friends, Church of Christ friends, and friends who professed no beliefs at all. Mom and Dad never even came close to criticizing these friends or acting as if we were any better because of what we believed. They never even pretended that they had it all figured out. They were simply products of grace. This was another wonderful gift for my sister and me because you could waste a lot of energy criticizing anyone or looking down your nose when a proper understanding of our condition before God could not be remedied by any effort or self-righteous act. It was all about grace and faith, and at the age of ten, I prayed that God would forgive me of my sins and trusted Christ with the rest of my life to the best of my understanding.

Anyone who examined my high school years closely would probably find long periods when there was no hint that I was a Christian other than my attendance at church. I am grateful that I dodged any drug, alcohol, or sexual train wrecks, but I was a self-centered, fun-loving goofball.

Sports dominated my life from third grade until the day I broke my neck. I played everything—baseball, football, basketball, golf, and track. Dad commented one time that if they ever took the air out of the balls, I would have no reason to attend school. When I wasn't on the athletic field, I was usually hunting or fishing with Daddy and some other friends. I rarely slowed down, but when I did, I typically had a guitar in my hands.

My friend Wes will occasionally talk about one of the last times he saw me before I broke my neck. He was picking up Kelly for a date, and evidently, I walked into the room, my guitar strategically placed, and played "Stairway to Heaven." My shorts were so short he believed I was wearing nothing but the guitar.

Daddy made sure that by the time I was ten years old, I could safely be trusted with a shotgun or a rifle and knew exactly how to work a hunting dog. Plus, I could fish and catch just about anything from a bream to a largemouth bass. One of my all-time favorite birthday gifts was a fly rod and an assortment of approximately fifty "popping bugs." That spring, I think I lost every single bug, but I learned how to fish with a fly rod as well as anyone.

When I first began to carry a shotgun, Dad not only "modeled" for me how to safely and properly operate it, but also constantly encouraged and coached me. On presenting me with what I believe was my very first shotgun, he simply said, "I want you to enjoy this as much as I always have. You have been taught from a very young age what is required. If I ever see or hear that you have done anything careless, I will take a sledgehammer and crush this gun into a thousand tiny pieces."

I knew he was serious.

In between seasons, my friends and I were constantly seeing how far we could go without getting into serious trouble. Usually, this involved going out and "chunking" stuff at moving objects. Stuff could be anything from water balloons to fireworks, and I think we managed to hit every moving target in our neighborhood.

I think the only long-term planning I ever did was trying to figure out what I was going to do on the weekend. Life was wonderful, and I was trying to squeeze as much fun into every day as time would allow.

And in hindsight, I had completely bought into the lie of what happiness and success looked like—wealth, health, a hundred intimate friends moving from party to party, superstardom on the athletic field, *Charlie's Angels* knocking at my door, and the most expensive hunting and fishing gear. And to think that today one of the things I miss the most is simply going somewhere alone with my guitar or a fishing pole.

The Coleman's dressed in our finest.

Pond hopping with Gary

Picking with Jenny

Happy Leon a.k.a. "don't mess with mom today!"

"Huckleberry" Scott

Track Days with Marcus and Taylor

BACK TO THE BOTTOM OF THE LAKE

So what would you be thinking? Severed spinal cord. Can't breathe. Can't move. Can't feel anything but a busted nose. Totally helpless. Certain that the next stop is eternity. What was I thinking? That I didn't want to drown? Was I in a panic for air? Did I want my momma? Was I thinking that I didn't want to die? Take a moment and think about what you might be thinking.

Prior to that moment, I thought there were basically two ways people approached imminent death: kicking and screaming headed for eternal punishment or like Jesus on the cross when He said, "It is finished!" I had done what I was called to do. I'd run my race. I'd run it well and was ready for my reward.

I heard a story about a young boy who approached an older man while the man was weeding his garden. He asked the older man how he would spend the rest of that day, if he knew he was going to die that very night. The man responded simply, "I would finish weeding my garden." I've always loved that story. To me, it describes a man so in tune with what he was created to do that when he faced death, he had no fences to mend, nothing left undone, no regrets, careless words, and opportunities missed. Just like Jesus on the cross—it is finished! *Ahhh!*

The people I admire the most will die totally spent, gas tanks on empty, squeezing every ounce out of everything God has given them. I have several friends who encourage me when I simply watch how they live, work, and play.

We have all heard the expression "There are no atheists in foxholes." I have never been a soldier, but I believe something wonderful can happen when a human being is faced with an all-consuming, horribly dangerous moment. The superficial in your life completely disappears, and you realize the only significant eternal truth: there is a God, and we need Him desperately. This kind of moment changes you forever. And to this very day, I thank God that I experienced this kind of moment on that particular day.

Facedown and helpless, I learned another way to head into eternity—embarrassed! I was certain I was about to meet my Creator, and I was embarrassed. I was blessed beyond all reason and took it all for granted. My parents and sister loved and supported me when I was at my most selfish. I professed to be a believer, but a close inspection of my life would reveal priorities that began and ended with me. I had been going hard and fast-pursuing a whole lot of trivial activities that had consumed and dominated my life.

I wasn't a bad kid. I was just a self-centered goofball. But when all is stripped away, it becomes perfectly clear what is meaningful, significant, and eternal. I had spent seventeen years chasing stuff and very little time on the significant. Yet at that moment, the thing in my life that I had neglected the most became the most important and powerful—my personal relationship with God.

I've learned over the years that a lot of folks are in wheelchairs through no fault of their own. Minding their own business, always cautious, and out of the blue, something totally unpredictable changes their life forever. But there are also a lot of folks in chairs because they were idiots. How many times have moms and dads said, "If you don't stop that, you're going to break your neck!"? It is no coincidence that the majority of spinal cord injuries happen to males between the ages of sixteen and twenty. I would place my "accident" somewhere in between—with a heavy lean toward the idiot column. You see, I had this defective mirror. When I looked in this mirror, I saw a seven-foot-tall, bulletproof man who was smarter than most of the folks I knew. Well, that kind of thinking will get you killed. In reality, I was an immature seventeen-year-old child.

That moment, facedown, I never prayed to live. Death was not my biggest fear. A surprise audit and accounting of my life to my Creator horrified and embarrassed me. I simply begged for forgiveness for the goof that I had become, and forgiveness was given. I could not have told you that Philippians 4:6–7 said, "Give your worries to the Lord. Don't worry about anything. And He will provide you with a peace that is beyond comprehension." I could not have told you that 1 John 1:9 said that if we will confess our sins and put our trust in God, He will clean us up. But by the time I was pulled out of the water, I knew with certainty—live or die—I was going to be fine.

One Flew over the Cuckoo's Nest

You guessed by now that I didn't die. A friend who was skiing with me gently rolled me over in the water and saved me from drowning. I consider his gentleness one of the first miracles. If I saw a friend lying face down in the water, I think I would jerk him out of there as quickly as I could. If he would've done that, he could have easily killed me. I immediately said that I thought I'd broken my neck, couldn't feel a thing other than what I have described as an electrical burning sensation, and was having a difficult time breathing. Whether you realize it or not, our abdomen muscles help us breathe. My breathing was tremendously labored because when my spinal cord was severed, the muscles in my chest and abdomen became dead weight, and for the first time in my life, my lungs were doing 100 percent of the work under a heavy load.

My friends gently lifted me and placed me in the back of a truck on an air mattress. The friend who had rolled me over in the water braced my head and neck in the bed of the truck by sitting where he could place his knees on both sides of my head.

We arrived at the Sardis Hospital's emergency room about twenty minutes later and were immediately greeted by a young emergency-room doctor who introduced me to my first of many "sharp or dull" examinations. Beginning with my toes and working his way up my body, the doctor began to aggressively "poke" me with a sharp instrument. After each poke, he would ask if I felt something sharp or dull. Well, I never even felt a thing until he reached the shoulder area. I can still remember when the realization of how serious this was occurred to my buddies. Everyone was in shock.

I was placed on a table where they began taking X-rays from various angles. After the first X-ray, I asked the doctor if it was "broken or jammed." You see, I could remember hearing about a boy who had done exactly what I had done and had walked away from it because he had simply jammed his neck and not damaged his cord. They took the second X-ray, and I asked again, "Broken or jammed?" The doctor told me that they could not see anything but were going to pull my shoulders down and take one more X-ray. When he returned to the table, I asked again, and he simply said that I needed to be transferred to Memphis for further tests. I pleaded, "Broken or jammed?" He gently replied that my cervical fourth and fifth vertebrae looked as if a stick of dynamite had blown them to a thousand pieces. Thanks a bunch, Doc.

I can easily remember my ride in the ambulance from Sardis, Mississippi, to Baptist Hospital in Memphis. I repeatedly told my friend Marilyn to please keep praying for me if I passed out or stopped breathing. The only sensation I was aware of was my labored breathing and the electrical burning sensations of my numb body, but I was also aware that the only part of my body that felt normal was my face.

By the time I arrived in Memphis at the Baptist Hospital emergency room, word had spread, and a crowd had arrived with my parents. They all greeted me when I was carried out of the ambulance. The only face I can still remember vividly is Dad's.

My friend Marilyn had made the call to my parents.

There is not a lot about that day that still wrecks my emotions. I can easily recall and talk about every mistake I made leading up to the accident and every bit of fun we had that weekend. I can remember the last time I stood in a shower. I can remember eating an excessive amount of tuna fish salad that weekend. I can remember marathon

Ping-Pong and pool matches. I can remember trying to ski with some of the younger children on top of my shoulders on Saturday and Sunday. I can remember using a trick ski, attempting to complete a flip while jumping the wake without wiping out, and everyone joking that I was fortunate not to damage something other than my pride. I have a picture of me sitting on a log just prior to my accident, and I can almost tell you everything I was thinking at that moment. The first football game of my senior year was scheduled for September 6, and I can clearly remember setting goals in my head about how much I wanted to weigh, how much I wanted to be able to lift, and how fast I would like my forty-yard-dash time to be before the summer was over. I was a real "deep" thinker!

I consider it a blessing and a source of strength when I remember the power and peace that I received when I was facedown, praying a totally dependent prayer. Without squeamishness, I remember all of the sounds and odd sensations, but I cannot think about "that" phone call. I cannot think about the note my sister was greeted with: "Your brother has broken his neck and is being taken to the hospital." I can barely type it. Thoughts of the call wreck me. I cannot imagine the horror of making the call or receiving the call. Can you ever recover from something like that? I caused 100 percent of that pain. I still see this pain on occasion when I look into the eyes of people who care about me—even with some of my new friends who didn't know me "BQ," before quadriplegia.

The shenanigans began immediately! After I was rolled into a private area of the emergency room, a nurse removed my ski vest and "Daisy Duke" shorts by cutting them off with a pair of scissors. This was the first of many moments when I realized I rapidly had to get over any bit of modesty or embarrassment that I might feel as a result of being totally dependent on someone who might be more concerned about helping me than about making sure all of my body parts were covered up. It simply isn't natural for a young man to be bathed, dressed, and taken care of by several young ladies. But it became a fact of life, and the truth of the matter is that females simply take better care of me than most males.

You cannot put a cast on your neck, so traction is the way they stabilize a broken neck. A doctor with a foreign accent began to describe what he was about to do to me. The only reason I mention his foreign accent is because what he was describing was so bizarre that I was certain I had to be misunderstanding. He would begin by shaving the sides of my head in order to create a clean space around my temples, where he could screw a metal device called "Crutchfield tongs" into the sides of my head. My first thought and question was how he would know when to stop. The idea of screwing any metal object into my skull had never even occurred to me. To my wonderful surprise, it really didn't hurt, but the noise created by metal being screwed into my head was unbelievable. The closest I can come to giving you a description of this sound would be to tell you to get a mouthful of very dry, stale Grape-Nuts cereal and start chewing! You can't even begin to hear yourself think.

The gatekeepers at the emergency room had told everyone that only family members would be permitted to see me. I could not move my head at all, so all I could do was stare at the ceiling. Every few seconds, a different familiar face would lean over me and say something like, "Hang in there, brother. We are right here!" There must have been six or seven different friends who immediately claimed to be my "brothers" when they were told that they could not see me because they were not family. When the doctor graphically described what he was about to do to me, all of my new "brothers," with the exception of one, decided that they would wait in the lobby.

It was a wonderful thing that my friend decided to stay. I became nauseated, and I was in danger of choking on my vomit because of the fact that I could not move my head. My friend Taylor and I were in a panic. As he was literally clearing my airway with his hands, he looked at an emergency-room nurse and yelled, "How do we help him?"

She unbelievably responded, "That is not my job." Somehow, that nurse ended up needing to change uniforms after she was covered with vomit. I underestimated my friends. I love you, Taylor.

I was transferred to a critical-care area of the hospital, where I would spend the next seven days. In addition to IVs, I had a tube that was inserted in my nose that ran all the way to my stomach in order to pump out everything that I had not digested (lots of tuna fish). I also had a Foley catheter inserted into my bladder. After they had literally screwed the "tongs" into my temples, they attached a cord that was run through a pulley at the head of my "circle" bed. At the end of this cord was fifteen pounds of weight to provide traction. The circle bed was designed to prevent the possibility of bedsores. Every two hours, I would be repositioned from lying faceup to lying facedown. As I was lying facedown, the attendants would literally bolt another stretcher to my back and proceed to flip me from one side to the other. This horrified me. You can imagine that the slightest tug on my tongs was not a good sensation. I lived in fear that an attendant would slip and accidentally drop the fifteen pounds. It actually happened on at least two occasions. If you know where to look, you can still see my scars. The screws in my head would never bother me unless someone was careless.

The pain of fifteen pounds stabilizing your forehead into even the softest material for two hours became unbearable. Within fifteen minutes after I was turned facedown, my forehead would begin to hurt worse than anything I had ever experienced.

I realize that the person least qualified to describe a critical area of the hospital is the patient. I have already told you that my view was limited to either faceup or facedown. Combine the limited view with a significant amount of drugs, and my testimony would certainly be kicked out of court. But there were several experiences that were so unusual, I am confident that I can describe them without much distortion. To begin, there was one nurse assigned to cover two patients. The other patient was a man named Fred. I had never met him and have no idea what he looked like, but I know that he was a patient because of a failed attempt by his wife to murder him. The wife actually escaped, and one evening, she dressed as a nurse and attempted to sneak in and finish the job. I was enjoying a wonderful moment of drug-induced sleep when Fred started screaming. Assuming Fred was just complaining, I started yelling at Fred, "Shut up. None of us want to be here!" Fred, if you are reading this, I apologize. I'm glad they caught her.

Once again, friends and family members were told that only family members were permitted to see me for a maximum of fifteen minutes every two or three hours. Well, when is the last time you tried to make a seventeen- or eighteen-year-old boy play by the rules? I was awakened one day by two voices encouraging me to wake up. When I opened my eyes, two friends dressed in white medical coats and holding clipboards were staring at me. My first thought was that I had been in a coma, my friends had already graduated from medical school, and they were now my doctors. I was more concerned about them being my doctors than I was concerned about being in a coma. I knew those boys weren't as smart as I wanted my doctors to be! Only when I noticed the tire gauge in one of their pockets did I realize what was happening.

My confusion was ever-present, but in addition to the above, I had a faulty heart monitor. I would drift asleep to a steady *beep ... beep ... beep*, and out of the blue, I would hear *beeeeeeeeeep!* All I knew was that sounded like my heart had stopped beating, and because of my lack of sensation, every time this happened, I just assumed I was dying.

Remembering my naïveté, I thought about everything that a person could do in a wheelchair. At least I can still play the guitar. I can still hunt and fish. I can play pool or Ping-Pong. Certainly, I'll be able to take care of myself. I was clueless and am actually glad that I did not know at that point what was in store for me.

REALITY SINKS IN, AND
THE BATTLE BEGINS!

Every spring and summer, spinal cord and brain injury rehab hospitals gain more customers than during any other time of the year. Eighty-five percent of these new injuries are males between the ages of sixteen and twenty-five. The Lamar Unit was no different. On my floor, there were approximately eight males between the ages of seventeen and twenty-five who had spinal cord injuries as a result of everything from motorcycle accidents to diving accidents. There was one girl a year older than me who had broken her back when the giant slide she and her friends were playing on collapsed. All of us had injured our spinal cords within ninety days of each other. That was about all we had in common. I was the youngest, and my injury was the most severe.

Oh, and I definitely should add that in addition to all of the patients who had injured their spinal cords, we shared the floor with patients who had traumatic brain injuries. This added another element of interest, because most of the folks with brain injuries could roam the halls, and occasionally, they would appear in your room in the middle of the night very confused. One young man fell in love with a life-size poster of a

Coppertone girl in a bikini that a friend had brought to my room. After I was awakened several nights by "Abe" sitting in my room and enjoying the company of the girl, I decided to relocate the poster to his room.

Approximately three weeks after my accident, a young doctor came to see me. He was a very kind, very concerned, nice young man. In a conversation I will always remember, he explained to me what all of the doctors believed to be true. He bluntly said that because of the severity of my injury, what I "had" at that particular moment physically was all that I could ever expect for the rest of my life. I completely understand the statement "Honesty is the best policy." But in hindsight, I have always had a problem with him being that blunt so soon, and I make it a policy every time I am asked to speak with newly injured people or their families to tell them not to believe when they are told what to expect for those suffering from spinal cord injuries.

At the time he told me this, I could not lift my arms at all and could only feel my face. This could easily have crushed my motivation for making any attempt at all in physical or occupational therapy. What if I was not a "believer" and had not been taught about faith and prayer? What if I had not been taught as a child to fight a good fight? What if my parents had not instilled in me a work ethic? What if I had not been driven by countless coaches to do and try more, even when my body was in pain and screamed to stop?

I have outlived countless numbers of friends and acquaintances with spinal cord injuries, and sometimes I wonder if a well-intentioned doctor or friend crushed their spirit or motivation with the cold, hard facts.

The day I broke my neck, I was around six feet tall and weighed 190 pounds. I had played competitive sports since I had been in the third grade, and I had spent many years in training, trying to become bigger, faster, and stronger. Physical challenges had always been very easy for me to accomplish. Even learning to ride a unicycle had only taken me a few moments. It is amazing how quickly years of effort can evaporate when you are no longer able to make an effort. My body began to atrophy so rapidly that I could literally see deterioration almost every day. My hands, which were thick with calluses, became a soft as a baby's within no time. By the time I left the hospital, I weighed in at a whopping 137 pounds, and I had grown an additional three inches!

After seven weeks, the tongs were removed from my head, and I was no longer in traction. I was so relieved! For forty-nine days, which is 1,176 hours, I had been flipped from facing straight down to facing straight up every two hours without exception. I had gone through this exercise 588 times, and I never overcame the fear that someone would carelessly drop the fifteen pounds while he or she was repositioning me and painfully dislodge the screws that were in my temples.

Traction had become claustrophobic. It was not only painful but also a challenge to eat, drink, brush my teeth, bathe, and wash my hair. I was also never alone. On a regular basis, I would play "possum" as if I were asleep just so I didn't have to talk with whoever was there. One night, I awoke and felt someone's hand around my face. I just wasn't in the mood to visit with anyone, so I acted as if I were still asleep. It was not until I realized my hand was having a muscle spasm that I discovered the hand I was feeling was my own. It was one of the first times that the realization of having no sensation was going to be a challenge. On another evening while I was facedown, I was startled when an arm passed quickly beside my head. Once again, the arm was mine, and it had fallen off the bed, where it had rested.

While in traction, the only therapists who visited daily were the hospital psychologists. I didn't want to be rude, but I just didn't cozy up to these folks. They would ask all of these warm and fuzzy questions in an attempt to get inside my head and emotions. They would show me these strange pictures and "inkblots tests," and they would tell me to express as best I could what came to mind. Well, that was none of their business, and I wasn't about to tell them the truth. In hindsight, I don't think I was being impolite. I was just afraid that if I truly expressed what I was feeling and thinking, I might have been transferred to the brain injury section. So I played the game and messed with them.

They were there every day at the regularly scheduled time, and I obviously couldn't run away, so I did my best to answer all of the questions. And on a regular basis, I would make up the silliest stories about those weird pictures and ink blots. I think they actually knew what I was doing because after one of the sessions, Dad came into the room and said something like, "I don't know what you've been telling those folks, but I'm not sure they will come see you again." Small victory for the guy with screws in his head!

So I was thrilled the day the screws and weights were removed. I immediately asked them to sit me upright, and I promptly passed out within ten seconds.

It was time for physical therapy. I was so weak at the beginning, all my therapy consisted of was gradually increasing the angle on a tilt table where I was lying in an attempt to increase the length of time I could sit upright without passing out. My first attempt lasted maybe three minutes before I lost consciousness. Within approximately six months, I had progressed to the point where I could occasionally sit upright for as long as two hours—occasionally.

To the casual observer, I was making little or no progress. I was more dependent than an infant.

It was hard to believe how quickly life could change. Ninety days earlier, I was spending a significant amount of time trying to increase my bench press and lower my forty-yard-dash time. Now I was a seventeen-year-old boy with less physical ability than a one-year-old baby. Frustration was a moment-by-moment battle. One split-second careless decision, and the people who love me and I would pay for the rest of my life.

As the days passed, something else began to bother me. Every morning in a rehab hospital, the newly injured patients compared notes with each other. Every day, a different person would excitedly tell everyone how they had gained a new sensation or the ability to move something that had been paralyzed the previous day. I really thought I was working harder than anyone in the hospital, but I was the only one who never could feel or see any progress. A victory for me was being able to sit in a chair for fifteen minutes without blacking out. I obviously did not know anything about spinal cord injuries. When a person damages their spinal cord, there is an attempt to determine if the cord is completely severed or only partially severed, and occasionally and wonderfully, sometimes it is only bruised. When someone is diagnosed as "complete," there is no hope whatsoever that any sensation or movement will be restored below the point of injury.

My injury was at the cervical level of the fourth and fifth vertebrae. If my cord was in fact completely severed, I could only hope for a limited sensation above my shoulders and little muscle movement beyond my biceps and shoulders. When someone is diagnosed as "incomplete," anything can happen. They were not really sure how to diagnose me, but there was a heavy lean toward complete.

Occasionally, some of the guys on my floor would all get in a bathroom behind closed doors and drink whiskey and smoke some dope. It frustrated me that I was working harder and praying harder than any time in my life and was still not seeing any results. I remember expressing my frustration with another patient when she replied, "You might as well go ahead and smoke some dope!"

I wish I would have learned a valuable lesson from this experience and never had another pity party. Even today when I focus on someone else's life, I end up in a place spiritually and emotionally that I shouldn't be. As a professing "believer," I know what can happen when you start comparing yourself to others. You either feel great about yourself by focusing on someone who is really struggling in life, or you feel miserable by focusing on someone who appears to be on easy street. I also have learned the hard way that at least in my life, God changes my heart before He changes my circumstances, and sometimes the circumstances never change. When my heart is right, my circumstances are irrelevant.

When a Christian makes this mistake, it's very easy to understand why we lose any influence with people who are nonbelievers. There were only a couple of patients who claimed to have any kind of faith at all. I was probably the most outspoken, but it's sad to think of the impact I could have made on the others on my floor. They certainly appeared more joyful and attractive to hang around with. There was a lot more joy in the dope-smoking bathroom than in my room.

In hindsight, I actually believe the therapists were even getting frustrated. I think most people in the occupational and physical therapy business are wonderful, caring people, or they wouldn't be in the business to begin with. But it is a whole lot more rewarding working with someone who is actually making progress.

I can remember there were some days in occupational therapy when a fork would be taped to my hand and I would sit in a corner with a plate of Play-Doh bits and pieces in front of me. Therapy that day consisted of trying to fork the individual pieces of Play-Doh and successfully bring them to my mouth. Quadriplegics and sharp objects do not go well together! I always thought that several pieces of steak would be much more motivating. There is no joy in attempting to fork Play-Doh.

My friends never stopped visiting. There was always a crowd of my friends all over the hospital every day. But unfortunately, when you become so self-centered and constantly throw yourself "pity parties," you end up missing some wonderful blessings. My friends were faithful, and they were doing everything they could to encourage me. All I could think about was how they were on the way to have fun at the lake, and I was looking forward to another day of battling Play-Doh. Even before I broke my neck, I had wasted many a day worrying about what I did not have instead of being grateful for everything I did have.

I was also getting unsolicited visits from a group of people with wonderful intentions, but in hindsight, I believe they were very misguided and caused quite a bit of pain. Several times a week, I would be awakened by a small group of people who believed that every "real" Christian was already provided with a healing for any physical ailment. They would stand over me while I was in bed, lay hands on me, and begin speaking in a language that was foreign to anything I had ever heard. They told me they were speaking in supernatural "tongues" and that if I had enough faith and confessed and repented of every sin according to the Bible, I would be healed. After they spoke in tongues, they would select a different body part and tell me to concentrate, pray, and try to wiggle a finger, for example. They would also point at a picture of me from that summer and tell me, "that" was what the abundant life looked like—strong, healthy, physically fit, sportin' Daisy Duke shorts!

They would tell me these wonderfully encouraging stories about all of these people who had been healed miraculously because they had

had enough faith. I was obviously the world's biggest loser when it came to faith. "Pray hard, Scott! You obviously don't have enough faith to heal your whole body, so let's just try for your pinky!" No joke. They literally said that to me.

I had been in a Baptist church all of my life, but I must confess that I had never really made an effort to study or learn much about Scripture. When they would quote verses that I was unfamiliar with, I had no basis to determine if the Scripture was being properly interpreted or was even being used in an appropriate context. I so desperately wanted to believe what they were saying was true! I don't believe I've ever prayed so intensely in my life. They would tell me and encourage me to try to confess every sin, and they even suggested that I needed to deal with any inappropriate thoughts that I may have had. Well, I was a pretty typical seventeen-year-old boy, and you can only imagine everything swimming around my head. It embarrasses me to this day everything I confessed to these people. But I was not making any physical progress. Spiritually, I was crashing.

I was so confused, and when I would ask almost any other minister who would visit if what these people were telling me was what the Bible taught, most declined to give a definitive answer or deal specifically with the verses in question. I was miserable and felt like the most faithless sinner.

In every church I have ever belonged to, there seems to be some very tough questions and issues that everyone is afraid to bring out into the light and deal with openly and honestly. How refreshing it would be to be around a group of confident, loving, nonjudgmental people who felt free to express all of their hurts, struggles, and questions. Even if everyone simply admitted, "This side of heaven, we will never know."

A young friend who was a new Christian was visiting one evening at the height of my frustration, and while we were talking, he reminded me I had told him that even as a new believer, he had the same Holy Spirit living in him that the apostle Paul and all of the writers of Scripture had. I decided to stop asking everyone else and open the

Bible myself, praying that the Holy Spirit would reveal to me what was true.

This friend who was nothing more than a rookie when it came to things of faith had found a passage in John 9 where the disciples had come to Jesus and ask him who had sinned and caused a man to be blind from birth. Isn't that the kind of question we frequently ask when we see someone suffering?

Jesus' reply says it plainly, "Neither this man nor his parents sinned. This happened so that the power of God would be displayed in his life."

God's word is more than sufficient and so wonderfully precious. I began studying the Bible myself, beginning with the verses they had been quoting to support their position.

To this day, I believe that God can heal me at any time, but I also know that in 2 Corinthians 12 when Paul asked that God remove a "thorn in his side," the Lord replied, "His grace was and is sufficient. Where we are weak, He demonstrates His strength." I learned to handle Scripture on my own instead of leaning on someone else to tell me what God's word said. I could now go and learn or discover on my own.

As painful as this experience was for me, my family, and my friends, I consider the whole experience a blessing, and hopefully, I have been able to comfort others who have experienced the same frustration and confusion over the years.

For several years after my accident, even though I was confident I understood what the Bible said regarding healing and some of the more unusual gifts that were present in the early church, I would really struggle and get embarrassed when confronted by someone who would boldly claim that if I had enough faith, God would heal me.

One beautiful day in college when everyone was gathered in an area on campus where there was a podium and anyone could stand and address the crowd about any topic, the speaker "called me out." Most of the time, no one would really pay attention to the speaker, but on this one day while I was sitting with a group of my friends, including my sister, I heard the speaker yell something like, "You in the wheelchair! Blond-haired boy in the wheelchair!"

Embarrassed, I whispered to my sister, "Please tell me there is another blond-haired boy in a wheelchair out here?" Unfortunately, he was talking to me.

So I turned around and looked at him from where I was sitting, and he yelled at the top of his lungs, "If you had any faith, you would not be in that wheelchair!"

If you have never felt the wrath of a big sister when her baby brother is being attacked publicly, consider yourself fortunate. The crowd, which had been paying little attention, became so quiet they could hear me grinding my teeth. Kelly shouted back at the unfortunate man, "If you had any faith at all, you wouldn't have all those pimples and certainly wouldn't need to be wearing glasses!" The crowd went wild.

My body had also become a complete mystery to me, and it was constantly changing. One moment, I thought I could feel something, and the next moment, nothing. One moment a muscle would move, the next moment, nothing again. Muscle spasms were frequent in every part of my body. Occasionally, even on a cool day, I would break out in a mysterious sweat. At times, it would only occur on one side of my body. My blood pressure was all over the place. Forget about bladder and bowel control. You're going to put what where? I quickly lost every ounce of modesty and confidence.

Because I was in the only local hospital with a spinal cord unit, we were frequently visited by student nurses who were learning everything they could about patients with spinal injury. One day, one of my favorite nurses asked if I would mind some students observing while I was catheterized. Why not! You can imagine how surprised I was when one of the students happened to be a friend of mine who was a couple of years older than I was in high school. We smiled at each other but never acknowledged in front of anyone else that we were friends.

If any medical person ever attempted to describe or explain autonomic dysreflexia, I evidently wasn't paying attention, or I didn't completely understand. "Dysreflexia" is a reality I live with every day. In layman's terms, I believe dysreflexia is God's way of giving me a warning when something potentially dangerous is happening to my body in an area where I may not have good sensation. Muscle spasms, chills, perspiration (sometimes on only one side of my body), and a spike in blood pressure are all symptoms of autonomic dysreflexia. It also seems that the more severe the episode, the more difficulty I have in trying to think and ask for help. Left untreated it can lead to a stroke or death. This was not only painful, but after every episode, I was a little more confused and a lot more discouraged about what my life had become. For years, I would have anxiety attacks if I strayed too far from someone I trusted to help in the event of an episode.

One fascinating tidbit about dysreflexia is though I have zero sensation in my right foot, if I sometimes happen to have a blister or unknowingly my shoe has a pebble or anything that would make me uncomfortable, I begin sweating like a "stuck hog" within a few minutes, exclusively on my left side. You could literally take a marker and draw a line straight down the middle of my nose and see that one side of my face would be completely soaked and the other would be dry as a bone. Remove the source of the pain, and within sixty seconds, the perspiration and dysreflexia disappear. Well, at least that's fascinating to me.

But again, dysreflexia can kill you.

My sister and parents were incredible, and I am still amazed that they treated me exactly the way I needed to be treated. We all cried and mourned over what our lives had become, but as my supporting cast, the greatest thing they gave to me was their expectations. Even in the midst of mourning, I was "expected" to get on with things. I certainly was willing to milk my accident for all it was worth, but my folks had other ideas. For example, before anyone in my class was scheduled to begin school, Mom and Dad arranged for me to have a tutor come to the hospital because I was "expected to graduate on time. No excuses."

My parents were also urged, pressured, and encouraged on a regular basis to sue the family that I was with when I broke my neck. Almost every other patient eventually sued and inevitably won a judgment of at least one million dollars, if not quite a bit more. It seems like common sense. Your son is seventeen years old, and the medical community is telling you that his ability to earn a living or take care of himself was going to be almost impossible. Some people could not believe that my parents would not do this for me.

There have been a few rough moments when the thought crosses my mind that it would've been nice to start out without ever having to worry about money again. But again, my parents had wisdom that could only be described as supernatural. To begin with, we were Christians and did not believe in suing, especially when it could hurt a friend. It was also an accident, and if anyone was to blame, it was me for making a bad decision and not being aware of how dangerous my actions were. But just as important, Mom and Dad were determined that I was going to do as much as I could with whatever God blessed me with. I know that I would never have worked as hard and studied as hard or as long if I had a huge bank account from the beginning. Mom and Dad's expectations for me had not changed. I may never be able to do anything even equivalent to a Wal-Mart greeter, but as long as they were alive, I was expected to never take a handout from the government or anybody else and contribute as much as I could to everything I put my hands on.

Approximately a year later when I was feeling really cocky about finishing my freshman year in college, I foolishly made the comment to Mom and Dad that I was taking the summer off! *Ha!* I was quickly told in no uncertain terms that if I was not enrolled in summer school, I would be expected to find a job. None of us had a clue what kind of job a person in my condition could do, but that did not change their expectations one bit. A part of my assignment was figuring it all out. It would have been so tempting to "mother" me.

I believe there is supernatural potential when expectations are combined with faithful prayers. When others expect more from you than you would even dare expect from yourself, you are carried to places that you never could have arrived by your own efforts. My family never attended a single pity party that I threw for myself and anyone who I could coax to come along.

One day, I was in an adjacent room while Mom was talking on the phone. I had no idea who she was talking to or who she was talking about when I heard her make the statement, "Well, he is severely handicapped." I was clueless who she was talking about, and later when I asked who she was referring to, I became livid when she said she was talking about me. I had no idea. No one had ever treated me that way, so I had no idea that anyone thought of me that way. I was furious! I said some very ugly things to my mother, but in a very short while, we were both hysterical with laughter. What a wonderful gift my family had given me. Large expectations! They did everything they could to keep me focused on the possibilities, not the impossibilities.

There were also some wonderful and hilarious moments in the hospital. The floor for spinal cord injuries was also the floor for brain injuries, and it was impossible at times to determine who was and wasn't brain-injured. Doctors included! There was one young man who very tragically had overdosed on alcohol and drugs and had literally fried his brain. Day in and day out, he would be beside me during physical and occupational therapy. It was difficult to tell when he was aware of his surroundings or completely unaware of anything at all. It became a daily challenge to try to encourage him to speak or smile or get any kind of reaction at all. One particular day when some of the hospital executives were getting a tour from the head of physical therapy, this young man was on a tilt table, and the therapists began to speak with him in an attempt to get a response. Evidently, he had had just about enough and screamed at the top of his lungs, "Chicken manure!" Needless to say I have cleaned his language up a bit, but you get the point. This was a young man who might say one word a week, and out of the blue, he yelled something like this in front of a huge crowd. What made the moment even more hysterical is that he looked at the physical therapist very lucidly and said, "My lips are chapped. I was hoping someone had some chicken poop lying around, and I was going to put some on my lips so I would stop licking them!" I think that was the only thing he said for about two weeks. This kind of stuff went on almost every day.

It also was a bit disconcerting when the night-shift nurse woke you so that you could take your sleeping pill and called you "Steve." Steve was the man with the brain injury down the hall. Do I take them, or do I protest?

There was also a wonderful group of people behind the scenes that constantly encouraged me. There was a precious black lady called "Mrs. Red" who worked the graveyard shift. Not only was she working at the worst time of the day, but her job was emptying urine bags, garbage cans, and any other mess that the other shifts had left behind. On a regular basis, I would wake to find her praying over me. Most of the time, I would not acknowledge that I was awake, because her prayers were so precious and so encouraging and I did not want to interrupt her. She would also very quietly sing spirituals that I knew was her way of loving and ministering to a young man she hardly knew. I wonder sometimes if she was actually an angel.

My first day in an electric wheelchair was also something I will never forget. For almost five months, I had totally depended on whoever was pushing my wheelchair to get me where I was going and even adjust me slightly when I was trying to have a conversation with someone. This can be incredibly frustrating, especially for a seventeen-year-old boy who was trying so desperately to become independent. As soon as I found the power button, I pointed the joystick in the direction where I felt like I could finally be alone. It just so happened that as I passed by the elevators, the doors opened, so I made a quick move into the elevator and was very pleased that I was about to "escape!" The only problem was I had not mastered the art of turning the wheelchair around or going backward. I think I rode the elevator for at least thirty minutes with my face in the corner in a position that I now recognize as what young parents called "time-out." Different people would get on the elevator and ask if I needed any help, and of course, my pride would only let me say, "No thanks! I'm just going to the next floor." Needless to say when I arrived back on my floor thirty or forty-five minutes later, I was in big trouble because no one knew where I had been. As humiliating as the corner was, it was the first time in months that I had been able to do something on my own and be alone. From that day forward, I would go somewhere that I knew I could be alone every chance I got.

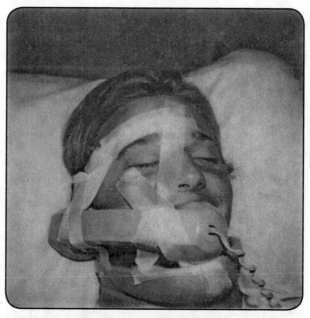

Kelly's idea of "Assistive Technology!"

"Gator skiing with Taylor" aka "Messing with Memaw"

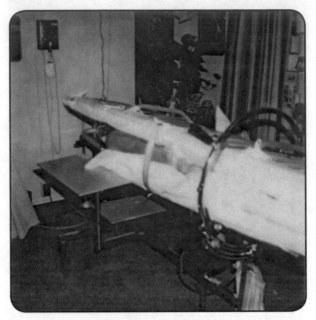

Stryker Frame a.k.a. "sandwich bed"

A visit from Sara and the future Mrs. Coleman

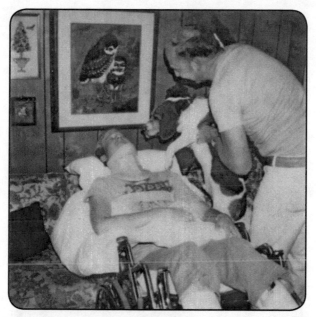

Dad showing me Dandy during the first week pass

From 187 lbs to 136 lbs in six months,
Busy the Kitty cat didn't mind!

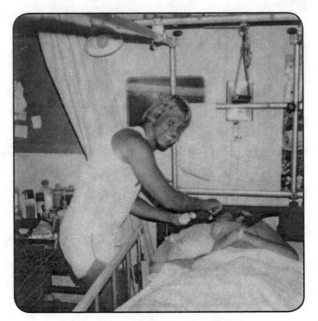

Taylor. Simply the best!

It's Not Your Battle!

Just prior to Christmas, my rehabilitation team (doctors, nurses, physical therapists, and occupational therapists) scheduled an evaluation meeting with my family to determine how much longer they recommended I stay in the hospital. The consensus by the "professionals" was that I needed another few months in the hospital in order to "be all that I could be." My parents had a different plan. They told the "team" that I was coming home for Christmas and I was never coming back again. Hallelujah! I was physically stable and was literally spending time in therapy attempting to either put a shirt on or take my shirt off. I was so hardheaded that I eventually learned to do this; however, it would take approximately an hour, and by the time I had successfully accomplished the task, I was unfit for polite company because of all the slobber on my shirt. Most of what I had learned to do required learning new tricks with my mouth. To this day, I still cannot dress myself, and honestly, I don't think it has reduced the quality of my life.

When I wasn't struggling with an attempt to manage a shirt, the occupational therapists were encouraging me to learn and enjoy their recommended new hobby for me, namely pottery. *Yoo-hoo!* I was so ready to escape.

Mom and Dad's argument was that I could learn everything I needed in the environment that I would be living in. It seems like common sense, doesn't it? Under much protest from the "professionals," I was going home for Christmas!

Physically, I was stable, but from an "ability" standpoint, I was pretty helpless. My lung capacity was terrible. Stamina was nonexistent. My chair would frequently need to be tilted back to prevent me from passing out. My sensation stopped at about my Adam's apple, and I could barely lift my arms. Less than a year earlier, I could bench press almost twice my weight.

I had completed the fall semester of my senior year in the hospital. As I have already explained, Mom and Dad were determined that I was going to graduate "on time" and had arranged for a tutor to meet with me in the hospital. I was scheduled to go back to high school after the Christmas break and complete my senior year. I was scared to death but thrilled to be leaving the hospital.

I attended a wonderful private high school. During the fall, my friends organized a week of "Scott" events with the goal of purchasing a fully equipped van for me.

At the time, friends and family were somehow transferring me from a manual chair into the front seat of a car. At its best, this was brutal, uncomfortable, and scary. Not only was I in constant fear of being dropped, but it was impossible for anyone helping me to keep my clothing in a presentable fashion. On a regular basis, I would expose the world to a view of Scott that nobody really wanted. I never was able to leave my home in my electric wheelchair, because it was impossible to transport the chair in a car.

So my friends organized a wonderful "Scott" week. On Monday, there was a "roller skate for Scott." On Wednesday, there was a "movie for Scott." On Friday night, my football jersey was retired, and after the game, my friends hosted a "Scott hop" and a "rock for Scott." My buddies raised over $25,000 and purchased a fully equipped wheelchair accessible van. There was enough money left over to help with some modifications at home. Unbelievable!

It was the perfect "reentry" experience for me. I knew everyone, and everyone knew me and cared for me. And they were always on the lookout for opportunities to help and encourage. I was still incredibly weak and could only sit upright in my wheelchair for a couple of hours without passing out, so my schedule had to be shortened quite a bit. I would typically sit by a friend in class who knew what to look for when I was on the verge of passing out. When I would give the signal, they would grab my wheelchair, leave the class, and help me recover. Many times, I would be sitting and enjoying the class with no distress whatsoever when a friend would grab me and head for the door. I became the easiest way to skip class in the history of our school!

I can also clearly remember the first time I had any indication of how serious dysreflexia could be. I was taking an oral exam where one teacher would read the question and the other would record my answer. Out of the blue, I began to very mildly perspire. In a few minutes, my vision was blurry, and I was sweating so much my hair became completely wet. In addition to muscle spasms, my head began to feel as if it were going to explode, and I was clueless and very embarrassed about what was happening. It was beginning to hurt so badly that I became very frightened, and I could not even communicate that I was in distress. I was wearing an external catheter at the time and happened to notice that it looked like it had blown up like a water balloon. Somehow I put everything together and realized that my bladder was distended and somehow was not able to drain. I panicked, and with my right hand, I simply hit the area as hard as I could and busted the catheter. Of course it was embarrassing to wet myself in public; however, the dysreflexia disappeared within thirty seconds, and even though I was humiliated, I learned a valuable lesson and was able somehow to finish the test.

In early spring, a group of my friends came to my parents with a sales pitch. "Scott isn't a baby. We are taking him camping this weekend at Sardis Lake, whether y'all like it or not!" They did not bother to ask me how I felt about it, but I couldn't help but think about the results from my last trip to Sardis. My parents never batted an eye, and they gave them their blessings.

I was on intermittent catheterization every four hours. Every one of them volunteered to learn exactly how it was done. I am still amazed by friends who volunteer and sometimes insist on learning how to help me with literally anything and everything. I often wonder if I would be so gracious if the tables were turned.

The spring of anyone's senior year in high school is one of the most exciting times in your life. Everyone is dreaming big dreams and making big plans. Every day, my friends were either getting accepted to colleges or being offered jobs. It seemed like everyone was headed for something wonderful. I was beginning to die inside. I was alone in a crowd, and no one knew it but me. During the daylight hours, I could "fake it" pretty good. At night, it was horrible.

A quadriplegic cannot "toss and turn" in bed. At bedtime, my parents would position me on my side with pillows, and in order to prevent any bedsores, they would come and change my position several times a night. I began thinking about my future and what I was going to do after graduation. Every night when the lights went out, I would begin listing everything I could and could not do. The "could nots" overwhelmed the "coulds!" I could only sit in a wheelchair for a couple of hours without passing out. I could not drive. I could not feel most of my body. I could not live by myself. I could not dress myself. I could not feed myself. I could not write. I could not control my bowels. I could not control my bladder. This list was a mile long.

I would start to pray, and this would lead to crying. I would start to cry, and this would lead to cussing. I was helpless and hopeless. I remember "telling" God what a mess my life was. I was angry with me, and I was angry with HIM. There was no doubt in my mind that I was responsible for my mess, but as a believer, didn't HE owe me a few things! Like a future?

I remember when I hit rock bottom and literally thought I might be losing my mind. I am way too much of a sissy to ever intentionally hurt myself, but I remember thinking even if I wanted to commit suicide, there was no way I could accomplish even that. Remember, I had not let anyone around me know exactly what was going on inside my heart. In the middle of the night, I cried out for Mom and Dad. This was not unusual because I would frequently have muscle spasms and would need for them to come rearrange my position. As soon as they entered the room, they knew this night was different. I angrily told them to crank me up in the bed, hand me my Bible, and leave me alone. I cannot imagine what they thought. I really could not even successfully turn the pages in a book.

They arranged me with a pillow in my lap and the Bible on top of the pillow. I had been in church all my life but had neglected any regular Bible study. I had no idea where to begin. Out of frustration and the inability to easily turn the pages, I would raise my right arm and smack the Bible in one direction or the other. I remembered hearing about a guy named Job from times in church. He had evidently had a few bad things happen to him. It took me forever to turn the pages to the beginning of his story. He was a train wreck—lost his family, his friends, his wealth, and his health. At the beginning of the book, he is sitting in a pile of ashes, scraping boils off his body with some broken pottery. His encouraging wife comes by and makes a sarcastic remark about his God. I know how I would've responded to that woman, and I was hoping Job was about to stick it to her. Instead, Job stuck with God. I hated Job! I wanted him to lash out. I wanted him to curse God and everyone around him. I wanted him to justify everything I was thinking and praying. I hated Job ... but I kept reading.

I remember thinking, *Yeah, but Job wasn't a seventeen-year-old quadriplegic with no future.* But I kept reading and literally wrestling with God. I have never audibly heard the voice of God, but that night, through the book of Job, I was reminded who God was and who I was. While I was telling God that I couldn't do this and I couldn't do that, He clearly spoke to me through His Word and said, "I never asked you to do any of that. All I ever asked was that you trust me." The Creator of the universe has given me the permission and the privilege of not worrying about my future. I am simply to trust Him with it.

My prayer that night and to this day has been, "Lord, forgive me for not keeping my eyes on you. I do not feel like it. The circumstances do not make sense to me. I am clueless. I am helpless. But I am going to trust you, and I am going to trust you with my today, my tomorrow, and my eternity."

One of my favorite Bible stories (2 Chronicles 20) is about a king whose kingdom is about to be overwhelmed and destroyed by a group of aggressors. When the king takes inventory, he realizes that he and his kingdom are helpless and hopeless. He cries out to the Lord and admits his fears and limitations, and at the end of his prayer, he prays the only thing that matters, "but our eyes are on *you!*"

At this point, the Lord answers, "It was not your battle to begin with. The battle is the Lords." Sit back, relax, and watch what I am going to do!

I was in the exact same place as King Jehoshaphat.

A part of me wishes that at this point of the story, I woke up with a "Benny Hinn" ending, completely healed—six feet tall, 190 pounds, and headed right back in the direction where I always thought I would go. But I believe my life has been so much richer than that. The following morning the "can't do" list had not changed, but the most important thing in my life had changed. My focus had changed from my limitations and inabilities to God's omnipotent power and possibilities.

I have learned that anyone who says, "Just take it one day at a time," is very fortunate to have never experienced a situation in which all you can do is hang on for the next moment. I have a new appreciation for the time when the Lord was teaching His disciples how to pray and He emphasized "daily" bread. Most of us have the luxury of not ever worrying about where our next meal will come from, but occasionally, life can be so rough that your next meal is the least of your worries.

THE POWER IN "DITCH DIGGING"

believe it is a mistake to pluck one particular verse or one particular story out of the Bible and build an entire life from it. Even though I rarely practiced this before I broke my neck, I have been taught from a very early age to consider everything in the Bible in context with everything else in the Bible. It would've been a mistake, and I would've missed so much if I had taken the Jehoshaphat story and simply sat in my room without ever making an effort on my own. "Let me know when the battle is over, Lord!" Sometimes the battles are a tremendous amount of fun.

There is another Bible story that I think goes hand in hand with the "not your battle" story, and it involves the same king, Jehoshaphat. Once again, he and his kingdom went out to battle and found themselves in a mess (2 Kings 3). They had traveled far from home and had completely run out of water. They immediately began to whine and moan that the Lord had led them out to the wilderness simply to die of thirst. When they finally cried out to God, His answer hit me square between the eyes. He told them to quit whining and start digging trenches. They would not see the wind blow, and they would not see the rain fall; however, God was going to fill those trenches! This did not make sense to them. There was not a cloud in the sky, and the wind revealed no indication that a storm was blowing in. They got to work and trusted God for the results. This is when God does His best work, and we receive His best blessings.

I have often fought battles that God never intended me to fight, and I have often neglected the work and the effort and the acts of faith that God blesses. I still struggle every day with knowing when to be still and when to start rolling. I have always heard that you can act your way into a feeling quicker than you can feel your way into an action. I have learned that God honors a step of faith in the direction of something that sometimes appears to lack any common sense or any hope of success.

My problem was I had no idea what my "trench digging" assignment was.

Personally, if I wait to "feel" like doing anything before I actually attempt to do it, I will never do it. The quadriplegic body rarely feels like doing anything. On second thought, that's a lie! I frequently feel like cussing, complaining, drinking, fighting, and wondering why in the world everyone who knows me doesn't come over here and join my pity party.

The morning after my encounter with Job, I had a peace and comfort that had been missing for a long time, but I was absolutely clueless about my future. And that was okay.! On "paper," I wasn't a very good prospect.

My morning prayer was simple: "Lord, I am going to start rolling and trust you to show up!" I was about to start digging trenches. My game plan did not involve "taking it a day at a time." My plan was "one moment at a time." I was clueless. I was powerless. But I was determined to keep my eyes on the Lord.

And I really can't remember, but if I was anything like I am today, I bet within a few hours, I was stinking it up and unfocused again; however, I had learned the awesome encouragement, peace, and power that is available at any moment and in any circumstance when I cry out to God. He is always faithful.

It is stunning to think about how much the world has changed since 1980. At the most, every home had approximately five TV channels.

No one could even imagine the Internet or why anyone would want a computer in the house. Cell phones were something that we saw on Saturday morning while we watched *The Jetsons* cartoon.

You get the picture, but for a seventeen-year-old quadriplegic, the world was a very unaccommodating place. As I began my "reentry" into the world, I quickly learned to appreciate all of the efforts toward accessibility that injured veterans have primarily made for themselves and everyone that is "rolling" through life. There was certainly a pioneer aspect for eighteen-year-old, cervical-level-of-the-fourth-and-fifth vertebrae quadriplegic. Every person in a wheelchair I met had chosen a path that was unattractive to me.

My family decided to take our first post-injury "road trip" right after I graduated from high school. We had family in Texas, so Texas, here we come! In Texas, I had the first of many of what we began to call "divine appointments. I had never met another quadriplegic that was my level or above. In other words, every other person with a spinal cord injury I had met had way more abilities than I did. One morning in Dallas, I was glancing at the morning paper when a story caught my eye. There was a local seventeen-year-old athlete who had broken his cervical level at the fourth and fifth vertebrae within the last year. I picked up the phone and called him. Well, my sister picked up the phone and called him for me.

We were almost identical in age, injury, and abilities ... or lack thereof. To this day, I have never met this man and have no idea how life has turned out for him, but the conversation was one of many that changed my life.

When I left the Lamar Unit, I swore to everyone who would listen that I would never darken the doors of another rehab hospital, so you can imagine my dismay when he began enthusiastically describing a spinal cord hospital that he was about to visit in Denver, Colorado. I thought he was crazy. Why would anyone after he spent the bulk of their senior year in a rehabilitation hospital volunteer to spend even another day in a place like that? I was not interested, but I listened anyway and quickly tried to forget about the conversation. I'm grateful my attempt to forget was unsuccessful.

When we returned from Texas, my family and I began to do some investigation about the Rocky Mountain spinal cord rehabilitation hospital known as Craig. The first thing we learned was that even if we were interested, their priority was on new injuries, and for someone like me (approximately one year post-injury), there was a long waiting list.

I honestly cannot remember what I heard or learned about Craig that made me want to visit. Maybe it was because I had never been to the Rocky Mountains. Maybe it was because the hospital emphasized recreation therapy as much as occupational therapy. Maybe it was because when I took serious inventory of my body, I was clueless about what to do next. Maybe it was because they told me that I did not have a chance getting admitted to the hospital within a reasonable amount of time. Well, I'm not sure who or what they thought I was praying to, but I was admitted for an evaluation within two weeks!

Craig was quadriplegic boot camp. I clearly remember my first impression of what was in store if I was accepted. When we were pulling into the parking lot for the first time, we noticed almost a dozen toppled wheelchairs on the lawn, with bodies lying all over the place. They were teaching paraplegics how to safely fall out of their wheelchairs.

I was admitted on an "evaluation" basis. For a week, they would run me through a gauntlet of tests in order to determine if they felt like they could do anything for me with a longer stay. Within a couple of days, they were making statements like, "We don't know how you've lasted a year." In their opinion, I was sitting in the wrong wheelchair. In their opinion, my bowel and bladder routines were either going to kill me or make me so miserable that I would wish to be dead. In their opinion, we had not been taught a proper, safe way to transfer from my chair. They also recognized my inability to do just about anything independently because I was so weak. They recommended an initial two-month stay.

I had never been away from home by myself, and while I was mustering up my most confident, brave face, I was freaked out on the inside as I watched my parents drive away.

I was incredibly lonely and homesick, but my time at Craig was a gift from God and changed my life. Craig was a blast! There are some people in the rehabilitation business with the attitude that "you are a quadriplegic, now start acting like one ... learn to enjoy pottery!" At Craig, I was constantly reminded that I was the same guy with the same desires as I was before I had broken my neck. I was just going to have to figure out how to participate differently.

I had participated in some of the most intense and taxing workouts and practices on the athletic field, but until then, I had never been driven, coached, and had my fanny kicked like I had at Craig. My physical therapist was a very cute young lady who could not have weighed more than a hundred pounds. She was tougher on me than any coach I have ever had. She immediately took my electric wheelchair away from me and said that therapy would begin when I rolled myself approximately a hundred feet from my room every morning to where I was scheduled for therapy. I learned that if I wanted to be on time, I sometimes needed to start rolling an hour and a half ahead of time. I loved it.

The abbreviated story of Craig is as follows: I entered, and I was not able to sit up right for even two hours without passing out. My daily schedule was planned around my bowels and bladder. I had zero confidence and was scared of my shadow. When I left approximately ninety days later, I could sit all day without passing out. I could do my own weight shifts to help prevent pressure sores. I could feed myself ... even soup. I learned to write with a pen by using my mouth. I learned to dial the phone with my tongue. I had figured out a way to shoot a shotgun again. I had spent many weekends sailing on a catamaran. I had met quadriplegics that had become teachers, doctors, lawyers, writers, anything they wanted to be!

Maybe the most important thing about Craig was the fact that the enthusiasm was contagious. It's hard to believe that a hospital can be so much fun, but at Craig, there was something fun going on every day. As serious as all of our injuries were, no one took themselves too seriously, including the doctors and therapists. I had never been in a place with so much diversity. There were people not only from all over the world but from all walks of life, faiths, and opinions.

I had one roommate who was a cowboy from a Western state . He was a slow-talking young man about my age whose injury was very similar to mine. He was painfully shy, and on a regular basis, I would get us both in trouble when I encouraged him to try something with me. At every rehab hospital, there is a program called "reentry." It is basically an opportunity to go to a variety of places and learn together what the experience of rolling through life in public is going to be.

I had visited a local amusement park on a previous trip with a group of other guys in wheelchairs and my mother. All I can really remember was that we had a really good time. My roommate did not want anything to do with any of this "reentry" stuff, so I was enlisted by some physical therapist to encourage him to go and volunteer to tag along with him. He agreed.

We were the only two quadriplegics participating in this trip. The rest were paraplegics who had strong upper bodies and could easily push manual wheelchairs. You cannot imagine the cussing he gave me when our bus parked approximately a quarter of a mile away from the entrance upon arrival, and it was all uphill. Our paraplegic "friends" rolled away laughing, knowing that it would be time to leave before we could ever manage to push our chairs to the entrance.

My roommate was livid, and we simply decided to sit in the parking lot for the next several hours. Within minutes, our plans changed. A busload of sorority girls from the University of Colorado arrived, and after my best sales pitch, we had our "pushing" companions for the rest of the day. The best part was the look on our paraplegic friends' faces as we pass them by several times during the rest of our visit.

Another roommate was a black man from South Florida who had broken his neck in a very unusual trucking accident. His injury occurred due to suffering whiplash when trying to connect a trailer to a faulty tractor truck. Not only had he been awarded a settlement from his employer, but he was further injured when the attendants in the emergency room dropped him from the x-ray table. The hospital had also provided him with a very large lump sum of cash. Mr. Jackson was a very wealthy man and was always treating us to something special.

I had been a member of the Fellowship of Christian Athletes from a very young age, but I had never heard of the Fellowship of Christian Cowboys. There were quite a few people in the hospital who had injured themselves while they had been working as cowboys. The Fellowship of Christian Cowboys was an ever-present source of encouragement and fun. One of the funniest things I ever witnessed was an injured cowboy who approached a doctor one day and said he felt like he was getting a bladder infection. The look on the doctor's face when he noticed a goldfish swimming around in his leg bag was priceless.

Life was really becoming a lot of fun again. I came away with the understanding that life was not going to be easy, but if I kept my focus and kept digging trenches, I was going to have an abundant life. If all of these other folks could do it, I could do it too.

A Body in Motion

I enrolled in the University of Memphis the following fall right on schedule, determined to get "it" done, whatever "it" was. I joke occasionally that my life verse should be Proverbs 26:11: "As a dog returns to his vomit, so does the fool to his foolishness!" I am amazed at how quickly I can get sidetracked and lose my focus, and it always begins with pride. Somehow even as a quadriplegic, I had acquired another faulty mirror. I became a cocky quadriplegic. I can do this. I can do this. I can do this! And I don't want a lot of help. Get out of my way. My focus was back on me and all of these cute little "circus act" tricks that I had learned to do back at Craig. I was determined to take every test completely on my own by writing with a pen in my mouth. It would take me anywhere from four to six hours to complete the occasional essay test. This isn't the most attractive thing you will ever try, but I really wanted to do it on my own.

In addition to everything that was going on with me physically, I experienced something my freshman year that I had never experienced before. I had no idea where I "fit." As I have mentioned, I went to a small high school, and unlike some schools, I soon learned there was a clear dividing line between groups—the athletes, the brains, the hoods, the nerds, the rednecks, etc. Well, at my high school, everyone just kind of hung around with everyone. If it would've been typical, I guess I would've fit somewhere in the "dumb jock" category, but at that time, I hadn't given this any thought.

A part of me really had no idea who I was on that huge campus. I basically just rolled around with my head down for a while.

Thank God that someone reached out to me almost every day. Sometimes it was a person I never knew existed in high school. Sometimes it was an athlete from another school who I had competed against. Sometimes it was a complete stranger who must have recognized the way I was feeling. But because of the graciousness of other students, I never thought about "fitting in" anymore.

The reality was I still needed more help than I had ever had in my life. Pride can train-wreck you and rob you of a lot of joy.

During my freshman year, I was in a psychology class with approximately two hundred other students. I began to notice that this very cute girl was always staring at me. When I would look up, she would smile and very bashfully turn away. Naturally, I began to think that this girl was really "digging" what she saw when she looked my way. I was so unsure of myself and insecure that I was not about to approach her, so this went on for weeks. One day, I looked up, and she was standing right beside me. That was when she said, "I hope this doesn't sound rude, but I've been watching you and wanted to ask a question."

I thought, *Game on!* Very sweetly, she looked at me and asked, "Are you a genius or something?" This was the last thing I expected to hear, so I don't think I responded at all. I just blankly stared at her. She saw my confusion and elaborated, "You cannot be more than fourteen or fifteen years old, and I was wondering why in the world you were in college." I was devastated! Now I think it's so funny that it always makes me smile.

My freshman year started out great with a lot of hope, and by the end of that year, I was self-centered; however, my "self" didn't even have close to what I required.

College was not a lot of fun for me, but by my senior year, my focus was back to where it should have been. There was a big part of me that wanted to stay in school forever because I knew finding employment was going to be a challenge.

I earned my degree in economics and finance with the goal of becoming employed in the investment business. The problem at the time of my graduation was that most Wall Street firms had a policy of not hiring anyone straight out of college. Everyone who interviewed me recommended I go out and get some "experience," with the exception of one man. Thank God for Richard Oates.

I am grateful that I was looking for a job before the Americans with Disabilities Act was passed. I believe that law has prevented many a disabled job candidate from finding employment. The law prevents the potential employer from asking some very thoughtful and relevant questions. Richard did not have a "politically correct" bone in his body. In every other interview, I was greeted by the potential employer with what I can only describe as a "deer in the headlights" look as soon as I rolled in the door. Not only was the interviewer faced with all of my usual stuff (My electric wheelchair... The splints I wear on my hands... The frequent muscle spasms I would have during a conversation) but something else mysteriously began happening while I was interviewing. Within minutes of beginning the interview, I would start sweating profusely, but only on the left side of my body. I had no idea what was happening, and the interviewer just assumed that I was incredibly nervous. Dysreflexia! But why was it always triggered during an interview and only on one side? When I say my entire left side was soaked with sweat, I mean I was drenched. We finally realized that my right "interview" shoe was rubbing me the wrong way. My body was responding to the pain and trying to give me a warning signal by the dysreflexia. These interviewers could not wait to get me out of the office.

The first thing Richard asked was, "What in the heck happened to you?" We hit it off immediately, and from the heart, he told me the good, the bad, *and* the ugly. Success in the brokerage industry was brutal for an able-bodied person. The odds were not in anyone's favor, and for me, it was going to be even tougher. But he kept asking questions, and we figured the thing out together. The agreement on the front end was that he was going to be as tough on me as he was with everyone else. He gave me an opportunity, even though I was really not sure that I would have given myself the same. Nationwide, my training class had fifty-five trainees. Within three years, only two of us were still in the business.

The trainee program at that time was "smiling and dialing." I was required to dial at least a hundred phone numbers every single day for the first year or however long it took to reach a minimum level of production. I had figured out a way that I could dial the phone with my tongue and arranged my desk in a way that I could reach what I needed and write with a pen in my mouth. I have said many times that the upside to this is that no one ever asked to borrow my phone or my pen.

As a trainee, I was required to travel frequently to New York and Philadelphia for further training. One incident is so comical that it is worth repeating. I was excited and nervous about my first trip to New York, and I was encouraged to do my best to make a great first impression. If it was possible to strut in a wheelchair, I was going to strut right into the home office! Have I mentioned that I have a problem with pride?

I was assured that transportation was not going to be an issue. After all, New York was the largest city in the world and could accommodate any traveler no matter what the circumstances. My first mistake was not arranging transportation myself. When I rolled off the plane, I immediately noticed two paramedics with a stretcher. They were holding a sign with my name on it, and I was hoping against hope that there was another Scott Coleman on the plane. There wasn't. At the time, there was a New York law that required that the "patient" riding in the ambulance be on the stretcher. You can just imagine my horror at the prospect of arriving at the home office in an ambulance on a stretcher. So much for first impressions! I used every newly acquired sales technique to make them break the law and allow me to stay in my wheelchair for the trip. There was one law that they absolutely would not break. While I was in the ambulance, they were required to run the lights and the siren. I certainly made a lasting impression with the home office. Exit pride ... stage left.

While I was smiling and dialing one evening, I came across a name from my past—Parrott. Linda Parrott was a friend I had met in Sunday school as a child, and I had grown up with her. We had actually dated a few times in high school, and our paths had crossed once or twice in college. When I was fourteen, she invited me to a Barry Manilow concert, and we had also been on a hayride together, so we definitely were more than just good friends. She claims today that at an early age, she not only wrote down but told many friends that she was going to marry me! I was clueless.

I can actually remember her visiting while I was still on the Stryker frame in the hospital. If a visitor happened to visit during the two hours that I was positioned facedown, the visitor had to lay on the floor under my bed in order to look me in the face. I still have a picture of Linda lying on the floor while she was visiting.

I cold-called her that evening at work, and it was the best call I ever made.

We talked a while and scheduled what she now refers to as a "Coke" date. A few nights later, she came to the office, we loaded me up in my van, and she drove us to the local Bennigan's. Immediately, I recognized that she treated me differently than anyone had treated me since my accident. There was no condescension. There was no pity. She didn't pat me on the head. It is tough to explain because so much of it is intangible, but she treated me like a man. I remember quickly falling in love with her so much that it hurt. I was constantly being "loved on" by friends and family members, but by the time Valentine's Day rolled around and she sent me a cross stitch that simply said, "I love you," I knew that I could not live without her loving me in a way that no one else could touch. She made me forget that I was in a wheelchair. I knew I was in trouble!

We were married approximately two years later. To this day, I am overwhelmed that I am married to Linda. I had to be completely honest with Linda from day one. I felt it necessary to tell her everything I feared and everything about my condition that was still a mystery. I knew how serious I was about her, but I loved her so much that I could not stand the thought of her committing to me before she knew the good, the bad, the ugly, and the unknown. We agreed it might be fun to figure out the unknown together.

Three or four years after the injury, I was still waking up to a different body every day. My muscle spasms were unpredictable, and my blood pressure was all over the place. I was unaware that some quadriplegics lose the ability to sweat when they are hot. We would be outside for an hour on a summer day, and I would run an elevated fever for the rest of the night. I was still trying to figure out the best way to accomplish even the simple things. Brushing my teeth was an evolving activity. Shaving was a 911 call just waiting to happen. Going to restaurants, ball games, church, or a drive in the country were always unpredictable, and these could unexpectedly introduce new challenges. Linda never flinched. She handled most things better than I did.

Not only was my physical condition a mystery, but as I have said, "on paper," I was a horrible prospect for just about anything. The day we were married, I was a broker trainee on full commission, without any clients, writing with a pen in my mouth and dialing the phone with my tongue. I wonder how many responses I would get if I posted all of this on an Internet dating site!

If Linda and I are not a "God thing," I do not know a couple that is.

Even after twenty-five years of marriage, she is still my best friend. I enjoy almost every day, but when my day is spent with Linda, it is always better.

First visit To Wall Street. Little did I know that the "business" of that street would be an avenue of so many blessings.

I Was Missing So Much and Sure I Would Have Missed Even More!

Approximately a year and a half after I broke my neck, my mom made the statement that we all "missed the miracle." What was she talking about? There wasn't a part of my body that I could wiggle or feel any more than I could within a month or two of breaking my neck. What was I missing?

If there is anyone who has had the blessing and the gift of more people from all over the world praying for them than me, I would like to meet them. From day one, my family and I were bombarded with phone calls, visits, cards, letters, and telegrams. All of them in one way or the other would say that "they were praying for a miracle!" In my mind, the "miracle" was a complete physical restoration of everything I was prior to that clumsy moment. So Mom had some explaining to do.

She said that if there was a competition for the "worst candidate in the history of the world to be happy and joyful while paralyzed in a wheelchair," it was Scott. To her, it was a much bigger miracle to know her son and remember that he never enjoyed doing anything sitting or lying down other than eating and sleeping and to look at him today and realize that in spite of it all, he was one of the most joyful and happy persons she knew. She was right.

I was not the kind of seventeen-year-old who would ever slow down long enough to "smell the bream bed." (Everyone with a subscription to the *Field & Stream* knows what I'm talking about.)

I was the guy who did not understand the law of diminishing returns. For example, after an exhausting weekend of waterskiing when everyone else was ready to pack up and go home, I had been the one who had insisted on one more trip around the lake. We know how that concluded.

For several years after an injury like mine, one just tries to survive. When there is realization that existence on the planet will continue for a while, the focus shifts from survival to independence. I am not going to live off the government or waste time in a nursing home. What is the absolute most that I can accomplish with the ability that I have retained? If fortunate enough to figure out a way to make a living, I knew that such circumstances would eventually lead me to wonder how to make a life. But more than that, I wondered, will there be fun and joy in life, or is it just going to be surviving?

Physically, spiritually, and emotionally, I was not the same person after my accident. From a recreational and leisure standpoint, I was almost identical, but my options were limited. Football, baseball, and track were out. Waterskiing was definitely out. I thought hunting and fishing were probably a long shot. I was grateful that I had always enjoyed reading, and I thought that through reading, I could get a lot of my "itches scratched." I was wrong, and thank heavens most of my friends and family members realized this way before I did.

GETTING BACK TO THE WILDERNESS

My friends were relentlessly determined to get me back in the woods. I am thrilled to write that today after years and years of trial and error, I can hunt and fish almost as well as I could before my accident. I could rarely hit the broadside of a barn before my accident, and I am proud to report that some things never change; however, this has not dampened my enthusiasm for hunting or fishing one bit. Dad has told me all my life that most of the fun ends "as soon as you pull the trigger," and he is absolutely right!

If it was all about the kill, certainly I would have quit trying to kill a turkey 20 years ago. I am still zero for life when it comes to Turkey hunting success, but I continue to go because it's an opportunity for me to be alone with some of my closest friends.

I am often asked by a nonhunter or by someone who doesn't fish why I enjoy these activities so much. I think it has more to do with being in the "wilderness" than it has to do with the activity of hunting or fishing. There is a passage in Mark where Jesus encourages His followers to "come into the wilderness and rest awhile." Even when I am participating in a strenuous activity, the wilderness is a place I can truly rest.

When is the last time and how often are you truly alone? When is the last time you even spent thirty minutes alone with a friend, totally inaccessible by any form of communication to the rest of the world? I believe you can learn more about a person in the wilderness, even if for only a short time, than you can know about the same person in other settings for several days in a row. Some of my most wonderfully intimate moments with Linda and other friends have happened while we were spending time in the wilderness, no interruptions. On a regular basis, Linda and I go to the "wilderness" in order to recharge our batteries.

On my wall, I have what I consider to be some trophy whitetail deer that I have "harvested." A part of me would much rather sit by the fireside and enjoy the success and the thrill that comes from helping someone else accomplish a hunting goal, but I have realized what motivates me and why I go and try to add another whitetail trophy to my wall.

For reasons that only they could explain, friends, loved ones, acquaintances, and complete strangers celebrate my victories in such a way that is nothing less than joyful. I think it probably has to do with the fact that when people learn my story, they realize that my entire life or at least the wonderful part of my life has been such a team effort.

I guess individual accomplishments are pretty cool, but I honestly cannot remember anything worthwhile I have ever achieved that I could've done by myself. It is simply more fun to share the struggle and the victory with those around you.

My friend Wes is an example of the kind of people I have in my life. I can't remember not knowing Wes Hoggard. He was several years older than I was when we were in school, and he was one of the guys who underclassmen kept their eyes on. Somehow even with the age difference, he "friended" me, as I hear it said today. After my accident, Wes would show up on a regular basis, and we would go "looking for ducks." I'm not sure that we ever found many ducks, but the fact that a friend would come and spend an afternoon with me riding through the countryside and talking or maybe not saying a single word was a form of rehabilitation that was like no other. He seemed to know that I occasionally needed to be "alone," and we would ride around forever, not saying much at all. Even before I broke my neck, Wes and I somehow managed to get trucks stuck on a regular basis. Well, why should this fun end simply because I was paralyzed from the neck down and could not walk for help when Wes would regularly take me places that we never should have been?

One day, Linda decided that she wanted to go with us "looking for ducks," so we all piled into my minivan and headed for the woods. Within no time at all, we are sitting in the middle of a wheat field with a flat tire and a brushfire headed in our direction! Calm Wes said that he could easily change the flat and get us out of this mess. Well, the jack fell over in the dirt with the van on top of it almost immediately. Very typically, Wes did get us out of this mess without any harm done, but he and I also got permission from Linda to spend a little money to either find or create a "proper" vehicle for us to use while we were looking for ducks.

Within months, I had the most wonderful off-road, fully equipped, camouflage, redneck golf cart! I started going places that I never imagined I could ever visit again. And within a year, someone stole this golf cart, and we never saw it again!

Enter "MacGyver" Wes to the rescue. I told him my budget and gave him the assignment of looking at everything available on the market in order to determine the best one to customize in a way that would accommodate my wheelchair. For several months, we would talk every day, and he was anything but encouraging. There was nothing out there that was going to work, and a few days before Christmas, he was going to take me and Linda to every ATV shop in the area to prove his point! I was not enthusiastic.

When Linda and I arrived at his office, he invited us in to "look at a tractor that he had been restoring." When I turned the corner, I could not believe my eyes. Wes and a group of friends had bought a brand-new Kawasaki mule, which they cut in half to move the gas tank and customized in a way that allowed me to roll on to the buggy, safely strap myself down, and go places no sane able-bodied person would go, much less a quadriplegic.

This vehicle has given me more joyful days in the woods with friends than I could even come close to explaining. I have also realized that what my friends' desired was more than wanting me to have a safe, enjoyable way to be in the woods. The buggy has given me the ability to spend more time with my friends and enjoying activities together that we all love. They wanted more time with me.

Typical friends. Typical of Wes.

I have always loved to hunt, but before my accident, I had zero interest in deer hunting because of the fact that you had to sit, be still, and wait! I actually had the opportunity to hunt deer in some fantastic places, but I was bored to death and never saw anything. Even after my accident, I was amazed when I compared notes with Linda. On several hunts Linda and I would be in the same woods at the same time but on different deer stands.. She would come back with stories about everything that she had seen, while I had not seen a single thing. What was up with that?

When this began to happen on a regular basis, I decided that we needed to sit side by side on our next trip to the woods. It became perfectly clear what was happening. When I was on the stand, I would daydream, talk to my partner, look at my feet and the trees, and eventually close my eyes from boredom. Linda's head was on a swivel! Her eyes and head were perpetual motion, alertly scanning back and forth. She had been told by a wise man to "look through the trees and not at the trees." My inability to move around became my primary deer hunting advantage over people who cannot sit still. The deer have a tremendous home-field advantage and can smell a moving Hunter and head for cover without ever being seen. From that day forward, I saw more wildlife than ever before.

I am still amazed that Linda had success whitetail hunting approximately four years before I put one on the wall—that was a long four years—but as of last year, I think I am ahead of her by a score of approximately ten to eight. I have no illusion that my lead will last for even one more deer season.

When I think about the wonderful moments spent with Linda while we were hunting, I often think that God has really piled on the blessings by giving me a mate who has grown to enjoy everything my dad and granddad taught me to love and cherish as a boy.

When I think about our early attempts to get back in the woods competitively, I am amazed that any of us continued to try. After many years of trial and error, I have adapted shooting equipment that is almost flawless now. A rifle mount attaches to my wheelchair, and I am able to pull the trigger by placing a device in my mouth and either "sipping," "puffing," or gently biting the mouth piece. It did take me almost ten years to even get a shot at a doe, and of course, I missed and bloodied my nose as a result of the recoil. Approximately three years later, the dumbest eight-point buck in all of southern Alabama walked out broadside to me at about fifty paces. I was so excited that I sipped instead of puffed when I was trying to pull my trigger and made more noise than you could possibly imagine, and I think out of sheer amusement, the deer just stood there and looked at me. I finally had a trophy for my wall! There was not a dry eye in camp for the rest of the weekend.

Every January for at least fifteen years, Linda and I had the blessing of spending the weekend in South Alabama at our beloved friend Corky Traylor's cabin. Linda and I would drive down with Dad and would spend two or three days hunting and enjoying the company of some of the best men we have ever known. Amazing how so few days spent in a remote place with people you love can recharge your batteries and remind you about what is important in life. Corky and our other friend Jere Dumas have been in heaven for several years, but our time with them gave Linda and me the desire to see if we could accomplish a twenty-five-year goal and find a place in the wilderness to build a cabin and spend time with friends.

As hard as we tried, we just could not find a way to do it comfortably. I knew that Linda and I would probably spend some time at the cabin alone, and it just made me nervous to think about being in the middle of nowhere and not having any backup for Linda.

Once again, out of the blue, a friend who at the time was practically a stranger enabled us to fulfill a dream. A wonderful man in North Mississippi had given Linda and me the privilege of hunting on his property. It was private. It was protected. And there was always help available to look out for us and assist Linda with some heavy lifting.

Our cabin has become my favorite place on the planet. There is no way in the world that Linda and I could express to "Mr. Bob" how much we appreciate and love him for being so gracious and thoughtful toward us. I frequently struggle to adequately express to him and other friends how much they mean to us, but I have come to the conclusion that maybe the best way to demonstrate how grateful we are is to attempt to take advantage of every opportunity to share every blessing Linda and I possess, and on a regular basis I tell them one of the reasons I am compelled to do this is because of what our friend Bob has done for us.

I love to ride through the woods very slowly and stare at everything from trees to critters. On a piece of property where I spend a tremendous amount of time, there is a very ugly sandpit that we would hurry through for almost a year in order to get to the next patch of pretty woods. One day, instead of focusing on what I consider a scar in the land, I happened to raise my eyes and look up beyond the area we were hurrying through. Amazing! When I changed my focus, when I lifted my eyes and looked beyond where I currently was, I saw the most incredible view from the ugly sandpit. I had never noticed that the area was elevated quite a bit and offered a spectacular view where you could see untouched forest for what had to be twenty or thirty miles.

What a wonderful experience. A place we rarely even considered became a place we intentionally spend time because we slowed down and changed our focus.

There have been multiple experiences and lessons I have had in the woods that I doubt ever would have happened while on my feet. On a visit to the Nashville zoo, Linda and I walked and rolled in front of the cheetah cage. After a few moments of rolling by the front of the cage, I nervously commented to Linda that I thought those big cats were following me! Of course, she thought I was paranoid and had a big chuckle. To prove my point, I reversed and headed in the direction where we had just rolled. Without a doubt, the entire pack of cheetahs followed me in the other direction. There is a verse in the Bible (1Peter

5:8) that says, "Be alert! Your enemy prowls around like a lion, looking for an opportunity to devour you." Come on! How many people have really ever feared being eaten by a lion?

A few years later in preparation for a trip to Rocky Mountain National Park, a friend e-mailed me an article about a paraplegic who was attacked by a lion while he was rolling on an accessible trail. I now understand and have a greater appreciation for the verse about being devoured. Until you have rolled through the woods as "prey," you have never had a day in your life when you were that *alert*.

I also had a great life lesson when a friend took me on my first predator hunt. It took a tremendous amount of convincing before I ever agreed to participate in the first place. It reminded me of the old joke about the conversation between two friends when they encountered a grizzly bear in the woods. One friend asks if the other thinks they can outrun the bear, and the other one replies that all he really has to do is out run his friend! Even a ninety-year-old can outrun me!

But my friend explained that we would be in an enclosed hunting blind that most varmints could not penetrate. We would have a weapon, and the call and decoy would be placed at least 150 feet away from us. I reluctantly agreed to go.

He arrived at our cabin after dark, looking like a redneck, Mossy Oak ninja. While he was gathering our gear, Linda asked if it would be okay if our twenty-five-pound Westie could come along. I exploded, "Linda, we are going predator hunting!" All she had heard was that we were going "varmint" hunting. The trip went downhill from there.

When we arrived at our hunting spot, the first discovery was that instead of the 150-foot predator call cord, we had somehow brought the thirty-foot cord. We were basically going to invite predators onto our front porch. The night started very successfully as far as I was concerned because we could not get anything to come anywhere close to us. After an hour or so, we decided to move and make one final attempt. The night was pitch-black, and we set our decoy and call approximately thirty feet away from where we were sitting and began to call. After several minutes, we would turn on a red lens spotlight to see if anything was in the area. Nothing! So we continued to try for another thirty minutes or so. On our final attempt, Linda suggested that our hunting companion shine the light a few feet to the right of where I was sitting. All I could see were red eyes, lots of fur, and a whole bunch of teeth. We all screamed like crazy folks. The spotlight was dropped, and unfortunately, so was our shotgun. We were sitting in pitch-black darkness with a dangerous predator way too close for comfort. I instantly called the night off and insisted that we immediately head for the cabin.

When we arrived safely back at the cabin, one of my hunting companions who will go unnamed commented, "Boy, I'm really surprised that happened." I could not keep my mouth shut and proceeded to give a sermon. I made a habit of praying daily, "Lord, help me to see trouble coming from a long way off." We had violated that when we realized how short our cord was. I also could not let the comment about being "surprised" go without providing my own commentary. Why would any of us be surprised? We went to an area where there were predators. We invited them to come see us. And we were totally unprepared.

We live in a noisy world. It is so easy not to recognize when danger or heartache is coming at you ninety miles an hour. Most of us could avoid so much pain if we would turn off the noise and take inventory. Slow down! Again, I pray every day that the Lord will help me see evil coming from a long way off.

There are so many life lessons you can learn from great hunters. On the day I am writing, I have never killed a turkey, but I enjoy turkey hunting as much as I enjoy anything else in the woods. A friend who typically has his limit before anyone every year and then proceeds to help all of his friends get their limit said to me one day that he had "only been out listening" on that particular morning when I asked if he had hunted. I was anxious to learn some of his secrets, so I began to pick his brain. It became clear to me why he was the most successful turkey hunter I knew. On some mornings, he simply went out and listened for the turkeys to gobble. If he was unsuccessful hearing anything, he would cry out to the turkey with either a gobble call or a crow call, almost begging to hear from the turkey.

To me, this described my relationship with God pretty closely. Some days, I simply need to be alone and quiet, and on many days, I need to cry out to the Lord and ask for Him to give me direction. Some days, it is so difficult to determine if I should be still and listen or constantly crying out. I believe both are essential to any intimate relationship. Unfortunately I do a lot more talking than listening.

The Whitfield Alabama Gang at Corky's

My biggest buck with Booth, Wes and Seth

Fun with John at dark corner

Varmint hunting with Katie (taking
picture), Daniel and "Mista Luke"

This is what happens when Linda doesn't get a turkey!

Abbeville eight point

Turkey hunting with the Tatum's

10 point buck with Shawn and a very interested "Scout"

Afternoon of Katie's first hunt and Luke's first buck with Daniel!

Corky's gang! Corky, Linda, Hitler, dad, Billy and Tom

Booth, four rifle shells, short buggy ride....Three slabs of bacon!

Abundant Joyful Adventure

Linda and I have always loved to travel, and we have had the pleasure of visiting some wonderful places. But once again, as with most things in a quadriplegic's life, it helps to have a pioneer spirit. One story will give you a flavor of dozens of impromptu "adventures" that we have survived.

We were planning a long weekend in Boston. Our travel planning typically begins several months prior to departure because of all of the special/accessible accommodations and transportation services that we will need. We were incredibly excited and had made our list and checked it twice.

I had only been to Boston once on business, so we were looking forward to seeing some of the historical sites and visiting with some of Linda's relatives in the Boston area. We tried to plan for every moment because of the limited time (four days) of our visit.

I completely understand and am sympathetic to the "deer in the headlights" expressions that we are greeted with when we roll up in all of our glory. "What in the world are we going to do with these two?" is written all over their faces. We have learned to politely and with an economy of words (carefully chosen) explain exactly what we will require from them to "pull this thing off!" We have actually gone as far as to acquire the Americans with Disabilities Act rule book on exactly what is required by the airlines. Linda knows how to get things done.

We arrived at the Memphis airport approximately two hours prior to departure in order to give everyone a heads-up that we were there and speak with everyone who was in charge so that everything would go smoothly and none of the other travelers would be inconvenienced by the extra assistance we were going to need. If only people would listen.

When the time came for us to board, they wanted us to transfer from my electric wheelchair to something called an "aisle chair." Without giving away too much information, my fanny is approximately two fannies too wide to sit successfully on this type of chair. If left unattended for even a second, I fall flat on my face, which is never any fun, and usually I end up mooning people if they happen to look in the direction of my fanny. Because of the impatient helpers that we are normally provided, this becomes an impossible juggling act for Linda. Five or six "helpers" are simultaneously grabbing body parts and equipment without listening to Linda at all. On this particular trip, she was trying to explain that we had purchased very expensive, sealed batteries that would not require disassembling my chair, and she even said, "And if you will look right here at the ADA rule book, you will see for yourself that we are telling you to the letter of the law!"

While she was busy attempting to protect something that was vital for our wonderfully planned weekend in Boston, they stopped holding me, and I rapidly headed to the floor. This was the best catch that Linda ever made. We were so frustrated and concerned about my physical well-being that we decided to ignore the chair and concentrate on successfully boarding the plane without major bodily harm. Surely, they could successfully load my chair into the belly of the plane, right?

I think we both breathed a sigh of relief when we were finally sitting safely in our assigned seats. I remember lamenting the fact that it was a shame we were both not rip-roaring drunks. It would've been so nice to be oblivious to everything that was happening.

Well, we sat ... and sat ... and waited for what must've been an hour or more when the pilot came over the intercom with an announcement. This is as close to what he said as I can remember: "This is the captain. May I have your attention? We apologize for the delay. Many of you probably noticed that there was a man in a wheelchair boarding the plane. We have had a problem with his wheelchair and will be departing as soon as possible."

When I heard the announcement, I looked down the aisle and saw a baggage handler approaching me with what looked like burnt battery cables. This is as close to what he said as I can remember: "Are you the man who had the wheelchair?" Heavy emphasis on *had!* The nice man across the aisle commented that he would sue them for everything we could get.

If only they would've listened to Linda, they could have prevented the fire that occurred in the belly of the plane when they attempted to disassemble my chair to make sure that all of us and our possessions arrived safely at our destination.

Linda ended up pushing me all over Boston. Unbelievable. I would've left me in the hotel room.

My sister was an employee of Delta Airlines at the time and was livid over the way Northwest Airlines had treated us. The wrath of a big sister is an awesome thing. She instructed us on exactly what to write and who to send it to. She was convinced that at a minimum, we would receive a free flight. We began making plans about where we wanted to travel on the free tickets that were sure to come. Several weeks after the letter had been sent to the president of Northwest, we received a letter from his secretary, "We are sorry for your inconvenience. Please except these two free beverage coupons you can use on your next flight with us." Yippee!

Over the years through trial and error, Linda and I had navigated trains, planes, automobiles, cruise ships, pontoon boats, Philadelphia, New York, Washington, the Rocky Mountains, the Caribbean, Kentucky, Annapolis, San Francisco, Texas, Florida, North Carolina, Virginia, Georgia, Arkansas, Missouri, Louisiana, Boston, Alabama, Chicago, and lots of other places we had no business traveling.

TRAVEL PICTURES

**Orange Beach with Kelly, Garret, Coleman,
Savannah, Tim, Travis, Linda, Mom and Dad**

Estes Park

Beach time with Linda

More of my girls....Savannah, Kelly, Linda, Lila and Kate

Rocky Mt. National Park with the Strange's

SLOW ENOUGH TO NOTICE

I do not have the ability to hurry. I have come to appreciate this as a blessing. It is much easier to recognize and appreciate things at ten miles an hour than it is at ninety miles an hour! I love the experience of either gazing while thinking about something or listening to someone when my whole perception suddenly changes. It's very similar to the puzzles we had as children—the longer we looked, the more things we recognized.

The quickest way to "Joy" for me is when I'm intentional about expressing gratitude. But it's a daily struggle. Recently while in Orange Beach, Alabama, I had the opportunity to spend some time alone and found a spot with not only an incredibly beautiful view, but the breeze was nothing less than perfect. After a few moments the "noise" I typically carry around everywhere I go began to disappear. It was one of those moments, in one of those spots, where I just became overwhelmed at God's goodness and beauty of His creation.

I started noticing young men and women "zip" by on a jet ski or a sailboat. I'm embarrassed to admit that I would occasionally feel a bit of jealousy or maybe self-pity, regretting I couldn't participate. I would capture the thought as quickly as I could and recover.

I remember thinking how wonderful I felt…inside and out.

My father-in-law walked by and decided to sit and visit with me for a while. My first thought was that I regretted no longer being alone. We talked for a minute and I began pointing at certain things I had noticed and was describing in great detail everything I was enjoying so much.

Suddenly I realized that instead of looking at anything I was directing him to, he was looking at me. What was happening? When I finally took a breath and stopped talking, he took the opportunity to tell me how much he appreciated how descriptive I was. He literally was unable to see anything beyond a few feet in front of him. My father-in-law has macular degeneration, and is losing his vision. He no longer can enjoy so much that he and I have always cherished.

It was one of those moments that the Lord frequently uses to bring my life back into focus. My father-in-law "Charlie" and I have always enjoyed reading about and discussing any topic we found fascinating. I honestly believe he became a doctor for the most noble reason. It had nothing to do with the financial rewards, and everything to do with the combination of his desire to genuinely help others, and "scratch the itch" God gave him to be perpetually curious. Soon he will no longer be able to read.

I've now added "eyesight" to my daily "gratitude" list.

I would love to be able to have one more conversation or spend one more day with several friends or family members who have passed away. I would do my best to go one mile an hour.

Before my accident, my circle of friends "looked" just about like me—primarily guys who either enjoyed athletics or outdoor activities, all of them within a few years of my age, very few girls other than occasional dates, and very few people who didn't share a lot of my interests. Today, I have some very close female friends, and friends in my life I may not have ever taken the time to get to know. I don't know what I would do without some of these folks.

I have become a person who is passionate when it comes to my friends. It is almost embarrassing how much I love these people. I frequently make an idiot of myself, but I love them so much that it physically hurts sometimes. I have lost the ability to be "cool." One of my best and oldest friends, a man whom I do not see enough, will give me the biggest hug and kiss when he sees me, no matter where we are or who is watching. Not exactly cool, but everyone is just going to have to get over it.

At seventeen, I was never going to slow down long enough to consider much of anything serious, meaningful, or eternal. I honestly cannot remember a single serious conversation I ever had with any of my friends prior to my accident. I look back and wonder at what age, if at all, I would have slowed down long enough to take inventory of my life. It scares me to think that it may have never happened. I certainly know many senior adults who are blinded to the fact that they are blessed beyond belief. I think I was headed down that road. One of my oldest friends had lost his father in a farming accident at a very early age, and to this day, it embarrasses me to think that I never stopped and considered what a life-changing moment that had to be for him. This same friend squeezes more out of life than just about anyone I know, but I wasn't paying attention back then.

One of the wonderful things that can happen through an accident like mine is a very sober examination of self and others, finding the ultimate reason you were created.

One friend who did not have a serious bone in his body shared with me one evening while I was still in traction that he had gotten on his knees the previous night and prayed, "Lord, this is Joe. I know you're probably asking, 'Joe who?' But I have a friend who needs Your help—"

Another friend refused to leave the hospital. He recognized that I had all the company I could handle, but more importantly, he realized that someone needed to be loving and caring for Kelly, Mom, and Dad. He was behind the scenes, but he was serving all of us in a way that was "otherworldly." He would also sneak into the hospital after hours so we could spend time together.

Some friends would write me letters or send me cards almost every day. I never saw a few others at the hospital, but I learned later that they were at home, taking care of laundry and the house while Mom and Dad were at the hospital.

One day, I was interviewed by a young physical therapist, and I had the blues because I was reminded how I looked from a young girl's perspective. At the end of the interview, she looked at me and commented, "Wow, you really can't do anything." She was simply being honest, but I was humiliated. That afternoon, I received a call from a friend I hadn't heard from in a while. He said, "I just need to tell you that I don't know if I ever would have considered anything eternal if you would not have broken your neck." That call changed my day, and the memory still encourages me today.

Even today, I have the most wonderful conversations with friends of all ages.

In the hospital, I spent many nights talking with my granddad, Pepaw, about his life. I learned things that I never knew and regret that all of it wasn't written down.

My sister is one of my best friends. We were always close, but the conversations I remember having with her during those early, post-injury days made me love her even more.

Simply watching and remembering Mom and Dad through everything fills me with a joyful gratitude that compels me even today to do everything I can to live up to their expectations. How did they keep going? How did they keep encouraging me? How did they get up every morning? Mom will tell you that her favorite Psalm became the passage in chapter 30:5, "There shall be joy in the morning." But the reality of my condition had a way of overwhelming much joy or hope. Even today, they are always around, ready to do anything needed.

There is a passage in the Bible (Hebrews 13:2) that encourages us to be careful how we treat strangers because sometimes we have "entertained angels unaware!" I have no idea if I have ever encountered an angel, but on a regular basis, a stranger comes along out of the blue and either gives a helping hand or an encouraging word.

One day, I was running late for an exam in college. Dad pulled into a handicap parking lot, and I carelessly rushed to board my wheelchair lift and promptly flipped out of my van and landed on the pavement, shoulders and headfirst. It completely ripped the sweater I was wearing off of my body. Out of the blue, a young man appeared and gently helped Dad lift me and my wheelchair into an upright position. Then he simply disappeared. We were in a big empty parking lot, and I'm telling you he was nowhere to be found. We wanted to thank him, but we never saw him again.

I wish I could find every stranger who has given me a hand, but that would be impossible. What I can do is take every opportunity to keep my radar on so I can recognize a person who might need a hand or an encouraging word. It is an awesome thing to have a complete stranger transform a horrible day into an impromptu joy session!

I remember many times thinking and saying that I would never have an office job or anything that required spending most of my day inside. I just wasn't "built" that way. And had I continued down that path, I would've missed one of the biggest blessings I have today. I have more than a job. I have more than a career. I have a calling.

The investment consulting business has not only provided me with the ability to take care of our family but given me the privilege and the joy of working for some of the most wonderful families that I could have ever known ... or likely would have never known had I not broken my neck. I spend every "workday" helping families invest their money in a way that can provide blessings for themselves and their loved ones.

I frequently hear people complaining about their jobs, bosses, and customers. I have no idea what they're talking about.

Linda and I were recently at a party with some of our closest friends. Wonderful people. Before the night was over, the men and women retreated to separate corners to discuss football, money, traveling, fashion, and the latest fads and acquisitions. From our separate corners, Linda and I kept making eye contact. She was as bored as I was with the conversation. It wasn't an immoral conversation. Some of the topics were interesting. But it was all trivial, and both of us recognized it in one another's face. We enjoyed the night, and we love our friends; however, there was just something missing. I commented later, "Linda, sometimes I thank God that I broke my neck." She knew exactly what I meant.

Shirley Temple Was Naïve or the Upside of Reaching the End of Me

Earlier in this book, I described the night of the "can't do" list. That night was approximately thirty two years ago, and I've got to admit that the list of "can't dos" hasn't changed very much. My physical abilities or inabilities haven't changed much. I go through bouts of battling dysreflexia, bladder infections, and muscle spasms pretty regularly. I am still almost totally dependent when it comes to most things that even three-year-olds can do for themselves. My fingers don't work at all. I basically have shoulder muscles and biceps, no triceps. Bowel management for anyone with a spinal cord injury becomes a tremendous burden for them and their caregivers.

Linda and I kept this from most people, but for approximately fifteen years, our lives were scheduled around the management of my bowels. Every other night, it would take anywhere from two to six hours, and some nights when we were convinced we had taken care of business and were totally exhausted, we would be awakened in the middle of the night. I would begin to experience dysreflexia because of the trauma that occurred almost every time we tried to "manage" my bowels. I honestly do not know how either one of us survived but by the grace of God.

Sometimes I still struggle and have never really figured out how to ask for help. While I was in the rehab hospital, a wonderful young intern had given me a pep talk on how I was going to have to not only educate most doctors I encountered but learn how to instruct people in the best way to help me. I didn't even know what I needed or how the need was going to be met. For the most part, this has never changed. At times, I can recognize that I'm beginning to experience dysreflexia but am clueless as to why or what to do about it, and the more severe the episode, the more hapless I am about asking for help. I don't know if I will ever figure this out, and this is one of the reasons I am overwhelmed when someone volunteers to help.

But the combination of trying to get the most out of what God has given me—failing miserably, I might add—and more importantly, the supporting cast that is always faithful, always encouraging, and continues to show up has given me the privilege of thirty wonderful years since the summer of 1980.

It is very easy to waste my story, coming away from it with the thought, "Thank God I'm not a quadriplegic!" Please do not miss the most important part of my story.

A few months before I broke my neck, I was watching a Shirley Temple movie with my sister. All I can remember is Shirley attempting to encourage a friend to "get up out of that wheelchair and walk!" using her best motivational skills. I cannot believe how naïve I was. I can remember thinking that if I ever ended up in a wheelchair, I would have "what it takes" to get back on my feet again.

All of us eventually reach the end of ourselves! Mine was obviously pretty dramatic, but all of us get to the same point at least once in our lives. There will come a day where none of us have "what it takes".

Recently and very typically while Linda and I were riding through the woods in my Kawasaki mule, I encouraged Linda to turn down an old logging road that we had never traveled before. Within seconds after we entered the road, we were stuck in the mud well over the wheels, hopeless and helpless to do anything on our own. Thinking I would use this as a "teaching" opportunity, I looked at Linda very sincerely and said, "We have reached the end of ourselves!"

Very sweetly, she replied, "What are you talking about we? I can easily walk out of here and be at the cabin in five minutes without you!" I really think she was serious for a few minutes.

But eventually, we all come to the point where we are alone. Our family can't help. Our friends can't help. And we can't even help ourselves. This is when your focus has to change and you have to lean totally on the Creator and beg Him to forgive you and take control of your life. The wonderful thing about this is that when you totally surrender everything you are and have, all the other "stuff" in life can be so wonderful. Your hurts do not hurt as badly, and your victories are so much more satisfying.

If I could give the most wonderful gift to everyone in my life that has graciously made my life wonderful, I think it would be the ability to live life to its fullest no matter what the circumstances ... any circumstance! To start every day overwhelmed with joy as a result of the realization that no matter what the circumstances, every day and every moment is a gift from God. Every day is an opportunity to be an ambassador of God and make an eternal difference in someone's life.

Unfortunately, I cannot give you this gift. That is my prayer for you, but that is only available from our Creator. Change your focus, and He will change your life.

Talent and ability have nothing to do with a wonderful life. Money and possessions have nothing to do with a wonderful life either. A successful, lucrative career has nothing to do with a wonderful life as well. Physical ability, health, and the lack of pain have nothing to do with a wonderful life. All of these can be blessings and can be the icing on the cake when the important part is taken care of.

It breaks my heart to see someone I love miserable, paralyzed with worry over "stuff." I am not unsympathetic to the horrific pain and health problems our corruptible bodies can suffer. But for believers, it is only temporary, and when we consider what He has prepared for us, our temporary troubles are not even worth considering.

If our relationship with our Creator is as it should be, our assets and blessings overwhelm any liabilities and hardships. There's no competition.

Frequently, I am asked that if I had the ability to flip a switch and never have broken my neck, would I flip that switch.

If it meant missing everything I have learned and everything I have experienced as a direct result of what started as a terrible summer day, I wouldn't change a thing, not for a bazillion dollars!

William Scott Coleman
Olive Branch, Mississippi
April 2012

Epilogue

Below is a letter I sent to my nephew, Coleman, on his seventeenth birthday. I hope and pray that at a minimum my life can serve as a warning of how important it is to not take for granted what and who God has given us. One careless decision can have eternal consequences. There are so many children in my life that I hope will learn from my mistakes and avoid unnecessary pain.

The letter was an attempt to tell my nephew how important he was to me and remind him to be alert.

April 12, 2011

Dear Coleman,

Linda asked me this morning if I could remember my seventeenth birthday. Vividly! Obviously, it was my last "able-bodied" birthday, and in fifty-four days, the world turned upside down.

I was running in a regional championship track meet that day. I was the only white kid in the hundred- and two-hundred-meter sprints. Ran my all-time best,

95

set a school record, and finished fourth ... or maybe fifth! I really can't remember, but I do remember not really caring because as soon as it was over, a buddy and I hit every farm pond in the area and fished until way after dark! I can remember thinking how great life was. I was on a roll, and things could only get better. They certainly did, but not in any way that I could have possibly imagined! It scares me to think where I may be today if everything I thought I needed to have a great life would have come true.

Horrifies me to think about what I might have missed! So with apologies to Brad Paisley, here is my "if I could write a letter to me ... on my seventeenth birthday!"

Dear Scott,

You have no idea the opportunities, privileges, and the blessings you have today and will have in the future.

On a regular basis, go somewhere by yourself and take inventory. Keep a journal. Read one chapter of Proverbs every day for the rest of your life.

Do whatever it takes to develop discipline in every area of your life. Be ruthless about this, and ask someone you trust to keep you accountable.

Don't assume your parents, sister, family members, and friends know how much you love them and appreciate them. Tell them and show them frequently in a variety of ways.

Treat everyone as if you might need them to catheterize you one day! You may have to ask that nerd for a loan one day!

Pray frequently that the Lord would help you to see danger/evil coming from a long way off.

Pray frequently for the ability to discern between the trivial and the meaningful or the eternal.

Pick your battles very carefully, and learn not to burn any calories on things out of your control.

Learn to listen significantly more than you talk. You can learn something from everyone.

Even if your biggest fear actually comes true, as long as your focus is on the Lord, there is no doubt that you will live the "abundant life."

Don't sacrifice your future for some temporary fun or comfort. Don't blink!

Sometimes it doesn't "feel" good to do the right thing. You can act your way into a feeling easier than you can feel your way into an action. Just start moving in the right direction.

Don't ever underestimate your "upside." If the Lord puts a desire in your heart, no matter how far-fetched or crazy others may think it is, go for it! Don't have any "small" goals.

The road less traveled is the only road worth traveling. Be willing to let God take you where He will. Don't be surprised when you end up somewhere more wonderful than you ever could have imagined.

And Scott, if an uncle who loves you very much and has lived long enough to make every mistake in the book writes you a letter, *pay attention!*

Love,

Me

PS: Mow a few more lawns and buy a hundred shares of Wal-Mart ASAP!★★★

Christmas at the Cabin with Savannah and Coleman

*So many wonderful, caring friends have helped me crunch through this attempt at putting this story on paper. Frequently while reminiscing and going over material, friends have commented that they would love to know what all of this was like from mom and dad's standpoint. All I know is that without the grace of God none of us would've survived and maybe my parents hurt worse than anyone.

Below is something that Dad wrote and sent to many friends when I was released from the hospital. I think it comes close to capturing where his heart was at that particular time.

First trip back to the site of my accident

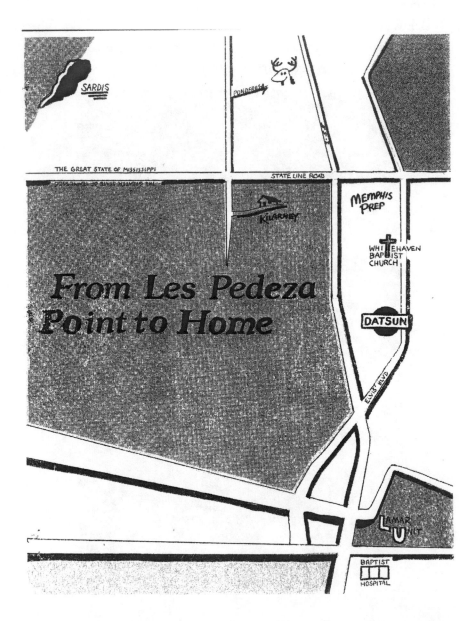

From
A Daddy's
Viewpoint

DEAR FRIENDS,

THERE IS SILENCE IN THE COLEMAN HOUSEHOLD FOR A
WHILE. RODNEY AND MARYLYLE, OUR SPECIAL FRIENDS FROM THE LAMAR
UNIT, HAVE JUST GONE TO WORK AFTER SPENDING THE NIGHT WITH
SCOTT TO WATCH A JOE E. BROWN MOVIE THAT CAME ON T.V. AT
5:00 THIS MORNING. THESE TWO PEOPLE ARE SOMETHING ELSE!
KELLY IS STILL ASLEEP AFTER A FRIDAY NIGHT DATE WITH BARRY
UNDERWOOD - THE YOUNG MAN SHE WAS WITH THE NIGHT OF SCOTT'S
ACCIDENT. LILA, BECAUSE IT'S DAYLIGHT AND YOU DON'T WASTE
DAYLIGHT HOURS, LEFT EARLY TO DO HER GROCERY SHOPPING. SO,
THAT LEAVES ME HERE TO DO SOME REFLECTING AND EVALUATING.

I DECIDED TO WRITE YOU ALL A NOTE AND EXPRESS
SOME OF THE MEMORIES I HAVE OVER THE PAST SIX MONTHS. AS
EACH OF YOU KNOW, THERE HAVE BEEN PEAKS AND THERE HAVE BEEN
VALLEYS -- BUT I SINCERELY PRAISE GOD -- THE PEAKS HAVE OVER-
SHADOWED THE LOW SPOTS.

PERMIT ME TO LET MY THOUGHTS RAMBLE -- AS EACH OF
YOU KNOW I'M CAPABLE OF DOING. ALSO, PLEASE FORGIVE MY SPELL-
ING.

"THINGS" HAVE ALWAYS BEEN IMPORTANT TO ME. LET ME
EXPLAIN! I HAVE ALWAYS HAD A JOB -- AT LEAST SINCE THE AGE
OF 13 OR 14. I FOUND OUT EARLY THAT IF YOU WANTED SOMETHING,
YOU COULD JUST WANT IT, OR YOU COULD GO GET A JOB AND BUY IT --
JUST THAT SIMPLE. IF YOUR TASTES RAN A LITTLE HIGH, YOU COULD
CHANGE JOBS FOR A BETTER ONE, OR GET A SECOND ONE. THERE WAS
ONE SUMMER IN BIRMINGHAM THAT I DELIVERED FOR MARTIN'S DRUG

102

STORE AND ALSO WORKED ACROSS THE STREET AT DAVE'S TEXACO.

I HEARD ABOUT A SITUATION AT RICKWOOD BASEBALL FIELD (B'HAM
BARONS), SO DURING ALL HOME GAMES I WOULD HIRE ANOTHER BOY TO
DELIVER FOR ME SO I COULD WORK THE SCOREBOARD. NEEDLESS TO
SAY, THAT ARRANGEMENT DIDN'T LAST THE ENTIRE SUMMER. BUT THAT'S
THE WAY IT'S BEEN AND QUICKLY LET ME SAY, I HAVE ENJOYED ALL OF
IT. I GOT MY FIRST CAR AT THE AGE OF FIFTEEN ($25.00 AND AN
AUTOMATIC .25 CAL PISTOL WAS THE TOTAL PAYMENT FOR THAT '36
FORD) I COULDN'T HAVE CARED LESS ABOUT SPORTS -- NOT THAT I
COULD HAVE BEEN A JOCK ANYHOW. I WANTED TO GO PLACES AND DO
THINGS -- THAT TOOK MONEY, SO I WORKED.

GOD HAS BLESSED ME THROUGH THE YEARS. I'VE CHANGED
JOBS SEVERAL TIMES WHILE MARRIED -- EACH SITUATION A LITTLE
BIT BETTER. AS THE YEARS PASSED, IT'S FUNNY HOW I DEVELOPED
PRIORITIES. I SAY IT'S FUNNY, BUT ACTUALLY IT'S SAD HOW YOU CAN
ALLOW YOUR PRIDE TO BLIND YOU OF THE REAL IMPORTANT THINGS IN
THIS LIFE. FOR EXAMPLE -- I LOVE HUNTING AND THE OUTDOORS --
I HAD TO HAVE THE BEST. NO ONE ELSE KNEW IT, BUT I WOULD NOT
LET A J. C. HIGGINS SHOTGUN IN MY HOUSE, IT HAD TO BE A REMINGTON,
WINCHESTER, BROWNING OR BETTER. I WOULD NOT WEAR ACME OR K-MART BOOTS
THEY HAD TO BE JUSTIN'S, RED WING, OR HERMAN SURVIVORS. I ORDERED
SCOTT'S FIRST PAIR OF GOOD BOOTS FROM L.L. BEAN COMPANY IN FREEPORT,
MAINE. I DIDN'T WANT A NON-REGISTERED BEAGLE NEAR MY PEN, IT HAD
TO BE REGISTERED AND FROM PROVEN STOCK. WHEN I BOUGHT KELLY AND
SCOTT THE JEEP -- IT COULDN'T BE JUST A JEEP -- BUT A RENEGADE
CJ-5. AND SO IT WENT!!!

BUT MY -- HOW YOUR PRIORITIES CAN CHANGE WITH ONE PHONE

CALL ON A HOT SUNDAY AFTERNOON -- ADVISING YOU THAT SOMEONE YOU
"WORSHIPPED" -- HAD BROKEN HIS NECK AND WAS BEING RUSHED TO THE
HOSPITAL.

LOOKING BACK OVER THE PREVIOUS MONTHS, I CAME TO
REALIZE THAT GOD HAD BEEN DEALING WITH ME -- HE HAD BEEN TRYING
TO GET MY ATTENTION. HE HAD BEEN DEALING WITH SCOTT ALSO, BUT AS
SCOTT AND I TALKED IN THE DAYS THAT FOLLOWED, WE NEVER CONSIDERED
HE WOULD HIT US WITH A BASEBALL BAT TO FINALLY GET HIS POINT ACROSS.

THINGS ARE CLEARER NOW! I KNOW THE MEANING OF LOVE.
I KNOW THAT WE ARE ALL IN GOD'S HANDS AND HE IS IN CONTROL.

IN THE MATERIAL THINGS OF LIFE, GOD PREPARED US FOR
THIS SITUATION! LET ME EXPLAIN------AS YOU ALL KNOW, LATE SUMMER/
EARLY FALL, IS TRADITIONALLY MY BUSY TIME. WE PREPARE FOR RUNNY
NOSES AND STOPPED UP HEADS. MANAGER'S MEETINGS AND SALES MEETINGS
TAKE PLACE. MUCH PLANNING AND PREPARATION! GOD SAW TO IT I
SUCCESSFULLY ATTENDED MY MEETINGS IN SNOWMASS, COLORADO AND
INNISBROOK, FLORIDA IN EARLY JUNE. HE HAS ALSO BLESSED ME WITH A
DISTRICT SALES TEAM OF CAPABLE-DEPENDABLE PEOPLE. SO MUCH FOR
THE BUSINESS! EARLY SPRING, WE TRADED THE JEEP FOR A MORE
ECONOMICAL, AIR CONDITIONED LITTLE DATSUN 200-SX. *ALL OF THIS
EXECUTED WELL BEFORE SCOTT'S BRUSH WITH DEATH. JUST HAPPENED
THAT WAY??? -- NO SIR -- IT WAS SIMPLY GOD'S PERFECT PLAN IN
PREPARING US FOR THOSE HOT - FRUSTRATING DAYS AHEAD.

BEFORE I GO FARTHER, LET ME TELL YOU ABOUT A LESSON
LEARNED THE FRIDAY AFTERNOON BEFORE THE ACCIDENT. MAYBE ALL OF US
PARENTS CAN LEARN AND "READJUST" FROM THE EXAMPLE I WANT TO SHARE:
I HAD ARRIVED HOME FROM FLORIDA ABOUT THIRTY MINUTES BEFORE SCOTT

CAME RUSHING IN FROM HIS JOB WITH BILL MAXWELL. I WAS IN MY
LITTLE OFFICE LOOKING OVER THE WEEK'S MAIL THAT HAD PILED UP
ON MY DESK. SCOTT HOLLERED TO ME AND WENT TO HIS ROOM TO CHANGE
AND PREPARE FOR HIS TRIP TO SARDIS. "DAD - COME IN HERE AND TELL
ME ABOUT YOUR WEEK IN FLORIDA." "I'M BUSY RIGHT NOW, SCOTT"
(JUST TWO DAYS LATER, HOW I WISHED THAT I COULD HAVE ERASED THOSE
WORDS) AFTER A FEW MINUTES SCOTT CAME TO MY DOOR AND FOR THE
SECOND TIME, "DAD - COME ON IN MY ROOM AND TELL ME ALL ABOUT WHAT
YOU DID." I THEN WENT IN AND SPENT A FEW MINUTES WITH SCOTT
CHITT-CHATTING BEFORE KEITH AND SUPER BOWL - THE DOG, CAME BY TO
PICK HIM UP. WHILE STANDING IN THE DRIVEWAY THAT AFTERNOON, SCOTT -
ALL 6', 185 LBS., KISSED ME GOODBY. WHAT A SPECIAL TREAT FOR ANY
DADDY! DON'T ANSWER IT OUT LOUD, BUT ANSWER THIS -- DO YOU TAKE
THE TIME - REALLY TAKE THE TIME - TO TALK AND LISTEN TO YOUR
BOY OR GIRL? STUDY ABOUT IT!! WHEN IS THE LAST TIME - IF EVER -
THAT YOU PRAYED WITH YOUR BOY OR GIRL?

I MENTIONED THAT I NOW KNOW THE REAL MEANING OF LOVE.
PERMIT ME TO EXPAND ON THIS:

LOVE IS A WONDERFUL COUPLE NAMED JIMMY AND MARILYN WHO
WERE SHARING THEIR BEAUTIFUL LODGE ON SARDIS LAKE WITH SCOTT WHEN
IT ALL BEGAN.

LOVE IS THAT SAME FAMILY SHARING MEMORABLE TIMES WITH
SCOTT DURING LAST HUNTING SEASON AT A PLACE CALLED THE PONDEROSA.

LOVE IS A SPECIAL FRIEND NAMED VIC WHO GENTLY HELPED
SCOTT WHEN THE SITUATION TOOK PLACE.

LOVE IS A LITTLE LADY IN CUT-OFF JEANS THAT RODE IN THE
EMERGENCY VEHICLE FROM NORTH PANOLA HOSPITAL TO BAPTIST IN MEMPHIS.

105

LOVE IS THE INNOCENCE OF SCOTT'S REMARKS: "ARE YOU SCARED "T"?" "DON'T WORRY MRS. AARON, I'LL PAY FOR THE LIFE PRESERVER."

LOVE IS CALLING JO ANN BUZARD - TOTALLY PRETTY AND TOTALLY CLASS - , THE HARBUCK'S SON-IN-LAW, AND MY COMPANY FRIEND IN LITTLE ROCK, TOM PACK - ASKING FOR PRAYERS - ADVISING THEM OF THE SITUATION. FROM THESE THREE CALLS, LOVE EXPRESSED ITSELF DURING THE NEXT HOURS IN THE FORM OF WELL OVER 100 FRIENDS IN THE EMERGENCY ROOM - LOVING US, HURTING WITH US, AND PRAYING FOR US. I WILL NOT TRY AND REMEMBER ALL THESE SPECIAL PEOPLE BUT I THINK I RECALL THE FRIENDS THAT WERE THERE EVEN BEFORE THE AMBULANCE ARRIVED. I BELIEVE IT WAS MARCUS CAIN, THE HARBUCKS, THE CARTERS, AND THE BALDRIDGES.

LOVE IS A BEAUTIFUL 6'-185 LB. SON - LOOKING UP FROM THE STRETCHER AT HIS MOTHER AND ME - CONCERNED BUT POSITIVE, "DON'T WORRY MOM AND DAD, I'M IN GOD'S HANDS."

LOVE IS GLANCING OUT IN THE WAITING ROOM TO SEE CHRISTIAN FRIENDS, HOLDING HANDS IN A CIRCLE, LIFTING SCOTT UP IN PRAYER.

LOVE IS A BLACK HAIRED BOY NAMED GARY, CONVINCING THE MAIN PEOPLE THAT HE WAS SCOTT'S BROTHER AND HE HAD TO SEE HIM -- AND HE DID. "SHAKE IT OFF SCOTT - WE'VE GOT TO GET READY FOR GERMANTOWN."

LOVE IS A BOY NAMED TAYLOR THAT 'TOOK CHARGE' IN SCOTT'S LITTLE ROOM - BATHING HIS FACE - JUST BEING THERE!

LOVE IS BOBBY DIXON.

LOVE IS JACK PANNELL AND ROBERT.

LOVE IS DR. LEWIS FERRELL - SO MUCH LOVE.

LOVE IS DAVID AND MAZIE BAILEY. MAZIE ALL DRESSED UP - BUT NOT TOO DRESSED UP TO TAKE CONTROL WHEN SCOTT BEGAN TO THROW-UP.

LOVE IS BILL MAXWELL AND HARRY LASHLEE.

LOVE IS THE RELATIONSHIP THAT EXISTS BETWEEN HARRY AND HIS SON MICHAEL.

LOVE IS RAWLEY CAIN.

LOVE IS THE LITTLE INTERN IN BLUE JEANS AND TOPSIDERS THAT CARED.

LOVE IS THE 'CREW' THAT MOVED SCOTT FROM THE EMERGENCY ROOM TO I.C.U. - TAYLOR, JOHNNIE SEAY, LESLIE MCNEER, LILA AND MYSELF.

LOVE IS TAYLOR AND JOE BROOKS - TAKING SPECIAL CARE OF KELLY.

LOVE IS KELLY AND SCOTT.

LOVE IS THE GROUP THAT STAYED THROUGHOUT THE FIRST LONG NIGHT WITH US - SITTING IN THE SMALL ROOM ON THE FLOOR.

LOVE IS THE PRAYERS OF BILL MAXWELL-BILL IS ONE OF THE MOST SPIRITUAL PEOPLE I HAVE EVER KNOWN. HE WAS ALSO SCOTT'S FIRST BASEBALL COACH AND GAVE SCOTT HIS FIRST SUMMER JOB. WHAT A BLESSING AND EXAMPLE HE HAS BEEN THROUGHOUT THE YEARS.

LOVE IS ANGELIA WILLIS, IN HER SWEET, QUITE WAY, SHOWING UP AT THE EXACT RIGHT TIME.

LOVE IS GRANDPARENTS AND FAMILY.

LOVE IS JEAN CAIN - A VERY SPECIAL LADY THAT SAW A SPECIAL NEED IN KELLY AND HANDLED IT WITH A SPECIAL LOVE.

LOVE IS TAYLOR - THAT WOULD NOT GO HOME.

LOVE IS A FRIEND THAT PRAYED ONE MORNING -
"GOD THIS IS_____, I REALIZE THAT YOU DON'T KNOW ME
VERY WELL AND MAYBE I SHOULDN'T BE BOTHERING YOU - BUT I'VE
GOT THIS FRIEND NAMED SCOTT AND HE IS IN BAD TROUBLE. GOD,
WOULD YOU PLEASE TAKE CARE OF HIM. THANK YOU, GOD".

LOVE IS BARRELS OF FRIED CHICKEN, HUGE PLATES OF
COLD CUTS, COUNTLESS DESSERT, MANY BANANA NUT LOAVES, AND
ON AND ON - THAT ARRIVED IN OUR HOME.

LOVE IS NANCY BALDRIDGE.

LOVE IS TOM AND JOY PACK CALLING AND CHECKING THAT
FIRST WEEK - EVEN THOUGH JOY WAS IN THE HOSPITAL UNDERGOING
SERIOUS SURGERY.

LOVE IS COACH PHILLIPS THAT WATCHED LILA AND SAW
TO IT THAT SHE ATE.

LOVE IS 'BUZZ' BUZBY - SEEING ME WALK WITH A SLIGHT
LIMP CAUSED BY STANDING ON MY FEET TOO LONG - AND GOING OUT,
GETTING ME SOME SPECIAL VITAMINS TO HELP MY CIRCULATION.

LOVE IS GLADYS BUZBY - ONE OF THE TRUE
PROFESSIONAL TEACHERS AROUND - SUPER LADY!

LOVE IS ALLOWING SCOTT AND I TO PRAY
TOGETHER IN THE EARLY MORNING HOURS. LOVE IS SHARING
WITH SCOTT YOUR MOST PERSONAL THOUGHTS.

LOVE IS A LITTLE DIETICIAN, JANE WOO, WHO UNDERSTOOD
ABOUT A TEENAGER'S EATING HABITS - AND MADE AVAILABLE MILK SHAKES,
FRENCH FRIES, HOT DOGS AND ANYTHING ELSE THAT SCOTT COULD HAVE
WANTED.

LOVE IS ART & SUE CONE - PARENTS, GRANDPARENTS, SUPER NEIGHBORS, AND SUPER FRIENDS!

LOVE IS MARY CARVER, A PERCEPTIVE, CARING MOTHER AND FRIEND.

LOVE IS THE EASON FAMILY FROM ARKANSAS - WAITING ON THE NEWS FROM THE OPERATING ROOM CONCERNING THEIR DADDY'S WELFARE.

LOVE IS BUNNY AND MARY LU - SO GENUINE AND SO SINCERE. MARY LU A COMPLETE MUSICAL ARTIST AND BUNNY, CERTAINLY ONE OF THE MOST DECENT PEOPLE TO COME ALONG.

LOVE IS TEENAGERS - BY THE DOZENS - ALL OVER THE PLACE - MAKING NOISE - LAUGHING - CRYING - PRAYING - CARING.

LOVE IS COACH OLLIE SMITH - LEAVING HIS WHEEL CHAIR DOWNSTAIRS BEFORE COMING TO SEE US.

LOVE IS TWO BOYS NAMED, BRUCE AND MARCUS THAT DONNED WHITE VET. JACKETS, CLIP BOARDS AND MADE IT PASSED THE SECURITY TO SCOTT'S BEDSIDE - JUST TO TELL HIM THEY LOVED HIM. THE AUTHORITIES DIDN'T SHARE MY DEFINITION.

LOVE IS 'TAYLOR AND COMPANY', TAKING TO THE STREETS TAPING CASSETTE INTERVIEWS TO BE SENT TO SCOTT.

LOVE IS GEORGE BUZARD - THE LUMBER MERCHANT - SO BLUNT BUT SUCH A GENUINE FRIEND.

LOVE IS MY FATHER-IN-LAW (PE-PAW) - JUST BEING THERE - A FRIEND FOR MANY YEARS.

LOVE IS A BEAUTIFUL GRANDMOTHER CAROLYN DIXON & HER GRANDBABY DIXIE.

LOVE IS MY MOTHER-IN-LAW (ME-MAW) - A SPECIAL GRANDMOTHER!

LOVE IS BOB AND EVELYN GIBSON.

LOVE IS PREACHERS, PRIESTS, DEACONS AND LAYMEN FROM
CHURCHES LITERALLY ALL OVER SHELBY COUNTY - ON THEIR KNEES,
PRAYING FOR SCOTT.

LOVE IS THE PRAYERS OF PAULA HAGOOD.

LOVE IS THE RELATIONSHIP BETWEEN FLOYD AND HIS
SON, JASON.

LOVE IS SPECIAL COTTAGE PRAYER MEETINGS FOR SCOTT
AND HIS FAMILY - HELD ALL OVER THE COMMUNITY.

LOVE IS THE PRAYERS OF JERRY RYAN.

LOVE IS A BLACK LADY THAT CAME UP TO ME IN THE HALL-
WAY ONE EARLY EVENING. "DO YOU KNOW THE FAMILY OF THAT BOY
NAMED SCOTT?" "YES, I DO." "PLEASE TELL THEM FOR ME THAT I AM
ON THE WAY TO MY CHURCH RIGHT NOW TO PRAY FOR HIM" "YES'M,
I'LL TELL THEM".

LOVE IS JACK PARNELL SHOWING UP AT MY HOME AT THE
RIGHT TIME ONE HOT MORNING AND REPAIRING OUR A/C UNIT - WITH
HIS SUIT AND TIE ON. JACK - ONE OF THE MOST TENDER-HEARTED,
LOVING, GIVING PEOPLE IN THIS STATE - BUT HE DOESN'T WANT IT TO
BE KNOWN! LOVES HIS FAMILY MORE THAN LIFE ITSELF! IS BLESSED
BY A GOOD WIFE AND TWO PRETTY TEENAGERS! SUPER GUY - SUPER
FRIEND - SUPER PERSON TO KNOW WHEN THE CHIPS ARE DOWN!!

LOVE IS MY NEIGHBOR, DOUG WALKER, GOING DOWN IN
THE FIELD TO PICK BLACKBERRIES SO ANN COULD MAKE ME A BIG PIE.

LOVE IS THE SPECIAL MASSES AND LIT CANDLES BY MY
CATHOLIC FRIENDS IN ST. LOUIS, CLEVELAND, CHICAGO, NEW JERSEY,
AND RIGHT HERE IN OUR CITY.

LOVE IS JACK AND NELL WIDDOWS - QUIET AND GENTLE - WHO HAD BEEN THERE AND UNDERSTOOD!

LOVE IS A LONG TIME SPECIAL FRIEND NAMED PHIL O'CONNOR WHO JUST "DROPPED BY" ONE NIGHT ON HIS WAY FROM CINCINNATI TO JACKSON, N. J.

LOVE IS CLYDE AND ALICE REGEL. CLYDE, QUIETLY PICKING UP THE BALL AND RUNNING/ALICE BACKING HIM UP.

LOVE IS MIKE VASSALLO, RON TESTA, AND HELEN NICHOLSON.

LOVE IS BOBBY DIXON - WHO IS AND WAS ALWAYS THERE.

LOVE IS BOBBY DIXON - WITH PROBLEMS OF HIS OWN - TAKING THE TIME TO GO WITH ME TO PRAY IN OUR DARKENED CHURCH SANTUARY. WE HAD REVIVAL THAT MORNING! I WENT BACK TO THAT SAME PLACE TWO OTHER TIMES BY MYSELF AND WAS QUIETLY JOINED BY BROTHER BOB AND THEN KEITH HAMM. ONE OF THESE DAYS, WHITE-HAVEN CHURCH WILL PROBABLY HAVE A SPECIAL - SAFE AND SERENE - PRAYER CHAPEL, THAT ONE COULD VISIT AT ANY HOUR. UNTIL THEN, TRY THE SANTUARY - YOU WILL RECEIVE A BLESSING!

LOVE IS MY NEPHEW - SO MUCH FEELING AND DEPTH - THAT SENT ME THE FOLLOWING"

"ONE SET OF FOOTPRINTS"

ONE NIGHT A MAN HAD A DREAM.

HE DREAMED HE WAS WALKING ALONG THE BEACH WITH THE LORD.

ACROSS THE SKY FLASHED SCENES FROM HIS LIFE.

FOR EACH SCENE, HE NOTICED TWO SETS OF FOOTPRINTS IN THE SAND...

ONE BELONGING TO HIM

AND THE OTHER TO THE LORD. WHEN THE LAST SCENE HAD FLASHED BEFORE HIM, HE LOOKED BACK AT THE FOOT-PRINTS AND NOTICED THAT MANY TIMES, ALONG THE PATH,

THERE WAS ONLY ONE SET OF FOOTPRINTS IN SAND.
HE ALSO NOTED THAT THIS HAPPENED DURING THE LOWEST AND SADDEST
TIMES IN HIS LIFE.
THIS REALLY BOTHERED HIM AND HE QUESTIONED THE LORD, "LORD,
YOU SAID THAT ONCE I DECIDED TO FOLLOW YOU, YOU WOULD WALK
WITH ME ALL THE WAY BUT, I NOTICED THAT, DURING THE MOST
TROUBLESOME TIMES OF MY LIFE, THERE WAS ONLY ONE SET OF
FOOTPRINTS. I DON'T UNDERSTAND WHY, WHEN I NEEDED YOU THE MOST,
YOU DESERTED ME." THE LORD REPLIED, "MY PRECIOUS, PRECIOUS
CHILD. I LOVE YOU AND WOULD NEVER LEAVE YOU. DURING THOSE TIMES
OF TRIAL AND SUFFERING, WHEN YOU SEE ONLY ONE SET OF FOOT-
PRINTS, IT WAS THEN THAT I CARRIED YOU."

                    BY DONALD COFF SMITH

                    With love,

                         Your Nephew Brad
                         (George)

        LOVE IS JACK PANNELL - AFTER WORKING AT HIS PLACE
ALL DAY AND SPENDING THE EVENING WITH US AT THE HOSPITAL -
COMING BACK AT 2:00 a.m., IN THE MORNING TO SIT WITH ME FOR A
WHILE LONGER.

        LOVE IS THE STAFF OF WHITEHAVEN BAPTIST LIBRARY -
A GROUP OF SWEET - LOVING LADIES.

        LOVE IS BOB AND ELAINE HAGGARD - WHO HAVE BEEN
THERE AND UNDERSTOOD.

        LOVE IS MIKE HAGGARD.

        LOVE IS OUR LONG TIME SO VERY SPECIAL FRIENDS,
JERE AND GLENDA - THAT ARE "WITH US" EVERY DAY.

LOVE IS ALL THOSE WONDERFUL PEOPLE THAT KEPT COMING
AND COMING.

LOVE IS A MUSIC MAN NAMED DOUG POPE - WITH SUIT AND
TIE, LAYING ON HIS BACK UNDER THE STRIKER FRAME TO TALK WITH
SCOTT.

LOVE IS THAT SAME MAN LEADING WHITEHAVEN BAPTIST IN
"VICTORY IN JESUS"

LOVE IS BRO. BOB.

LOVE IS NORVIN FORRESTER.

LOVE IS SUZANNE TERRY - WHO IS JUST AS PRETTY ON
THE INSIDE AS SHE IS ON THE OUTSIDE.

LOVE IS CONRAD AND OLEDA HUDDLESTON.

LOVE IS COACH BILL BRETHERICK - A BUSY MAN, BUT NOT
TOO BUSY TO CARE AND BE THERE. BILL 'KNEW' AND TOOK TIME WITH
KELLY.

LOVE IS DOZENS OF BROWNIES AND LOTS OF FRIED CHICKEN
FROM THE BADDOUR KITCHEN.

LOVE IS BILL NIPPER, JIM CRAIN, AND BROOKS LAMMY -
CUTTING OUR GRASS ON A HOT JULY 4TH.

LOVE IS LAMAR AND PEGGY HARTSOG, BOTH WITH FEELING
AND DEPTH.

LOVE IS BETH AND JESS FLANNERY WHO HURT WITH US.

LOVE IS CAROL AND CHUCK - SHERRY AND KEITH - ONE OF
THE CLOSEST FAMILIES I KNOW.

LOVE IS JOY AND GEORGE - LOTS OF FEELING - DEPTH
AND COMMON SENSE.

A SPECIAL LOVE IS MY LITTLE SISTER-IN-LAW, PAM, (AUNT PAM)
WHO FLEW UP TWICE TO BE HERE AND HELP.

LOVE IS THE NIGHT SHIFT CHAPLIN - WHO KNEW WHAT TO
SAY.

LOVE IS PEOPLE FROM YEARS AGO - CALLING AND CHECKING -
CHARLES HIGHTOWER AND BARBARA MITCHELL.

LOVE IS JIMMY, MARYLYN, VIC, KEITH, LEIGH AND
CHARLIE..

LOVE IS MR. BILL WALKER OF WALKER DRUG COMPANY -
WHO HAS NEVER BEEN TOO BUSY TO STOP AND LISTEN - IN GOOD TIMES
AND BAD.

LOVE IS PAT JEANES (PROCTOR ZIBBLE) WHO JUST HAPPENED
TO BE BROWSING THROUGH THE BAPTIST BOOK STORE - FOUND A STACK
OF BOOKS AND BOUGHT THE COLEMAN'S A SPECIAL ONE.

LOVE IS THE READY SMILE ON MRS. AL ROWE'
FACE

LOVE IS A SPECIAL YOUNG LADY - PAM HARRISON -
FOR A LONG TIME A FRIEND OF KELLY'S - ALWAYS SMILING,
LAUGHING, AND LIGHT-HEARTED.

LOVE IS DR. JAMES ROBINSON - A FRIEND OF
KELLY'S FROM DELTA STATE - SENSITIVE, ATTENTIVE AND
CARING.

LOVE IS BETH SNOZNIK - A GOOD FRIEND - AND A
SOUTHERN LADY.

LOVE IS JIM & PEGGY MURPHY - SEEING TO IT THAT WE
HAD OUR WINTER'S SUPPLY OF FIREWOOD.

LOVE IS BILL & JO DORSEY - THEIR UNDERSTANDING -
THEIR CONCERN.

LOVE IS MY MOTHER'S FEELING FOR SCOTT. "SCOTT HAS ALWAYS
BEEN SPECIAL TO ME."

LOVE IS A GIANT OF A MAN CALLED MR. CARTWRIGHT —
WHO WAS THE FIRST PERSON WE SAW FROM THE LAMAR UNIT. SUCH
A LOUD BARK BUT, SO GENTLE AND SO PROFESSIONAL.

LOVE IS HARRY LASHLEE, WHO TOOK ME TO MORRISON'S
FOR THE FIRST MEAL I HAD IN MANY DAYS. I BELIEVE HARRY
WOULD GIVE YOU THE SHIRT OFF HIS BACK.

LOVE IS BILL MAXWELL, WHO WOULD COME BY — BRIEFLY
SHARE A SCRIPTURE WITH SCOTT — AND THEN BE ON HIS WAY. A
TRUE FRIEND.

LOVE IS SCOTT ON THE STRIKER FRAME — WITH THAT
CROOKED GRIN ON HIS FACE.

LOVE IS KELLY, WHO CONTINUED TO HURT FOR HER BROTHER.

LOVE IS TEARS SHED BY SCOTT WHEN HE FOUND OUT ABOUT
CHARLIE'S PHYSICAL CONDITION.

LOVE IS A MOTHER SUCH AS LILA, WHO HAS SPENT MANY
HOURS ON HER FEET AT THE LAMAR UNIT — LOVING, HURTING, PRAYING,
DOING WITHOUT PROPER FOOD, PROPER REST, AND STILL TAKING THE
TIME TO CARE FOR KELLY.

LOVE IS THOSE TRUSTED FRIENDS THAT RELIEVED US
FROM TIME TO TIME.

LOVE IS JERRY VASTBINDER — SCOTT'S FIRST
ROOMMATE.

LOVE IS THE SPECIAL PEOPLE WITH MY COMPANY WHO
WERE THERE AND CONTINUE TO BE THERE.

LOVE IS OUR LONG TIME FRIEND KEN LOGAN — HUNTER

STREET BAPTIST'S SPECIAL ENVOY. TRULY A FRIEND AND SPIRIT-
UAL PERSON.

LOVE IS THE VISITING PASTOR FROM FIRST ASSEMBLY
CHURCH, REVEREND JONES.

LOVE IS THE RELATIONSHIPS THAT HAVE DEVELOPED OVER
THE MONTHS AT THE LAMAR UNIT. MRS. CHANDLER - THE SECRETARY
WHO LOST HER ONLY SON IN THAT VIET NAM SITUATION. MRS.
MINDEZ, THE LITTLE TRAINING NURSE WHO SHARED A WEALTH OF
INFORMATION WITH US CONCERNING THE CARE OF SCOTT. MRS.
FERLONIE - A JOLLY CARING PERSON. MRS. MOSS, A FRIENDLY
KNOWLEDGEABLE PROFESSIONAL. MRS. ADKINS, A BUSY,BUT CON-
CERNED LADY. GARY COLE, ONE OF THE BEST.

LOVE IS THE BLACK NURSES ATTENDANT THAT I OVER-
HEARD PRAYING IN SCOTT'S ROOM ONE MORNING ABOUT 3:00 A.M.
"DEAR SWEET JESUS - WE LOVE YOU, WE PRAISE YOUR HOLY NAME -
DEAR JESUS, I LIFT SCOTT UP TO YOU, I CLAIM YOUR PROMISES,
I BEG YOU TO HEAL HIS BODY. JESUS, THANK YOU FOR THE STILL-
NESS OF THIS MORNING. THANK YOU JESUS."

LOVE IS MARYLYLE, RODNEY, AND VIRGINIA. ONE FROM
VICKSBURG, ONE FROM FORREST CITY, AND ONE FROM SOUTH GEORGIA.
ALL THREE WITH SEPARATE BACKGROUNDS AND DIFFERENT PERSONALITIES -
ALL THREE SO VERY SPECIAL.

LOVE IS THOSE FRIENDS THAT SAW TO IT THAT SCOTT
RECEIVED AUTOGRAPHED PICTURES FROM JOHNNIE MAJORS, DOUG
BARFIELD, STEVE SLOAN, BEAR BRYANT, AND LU HOLTZ.

LOVE IS A PERSONAL LETTER FROM COMMISSIONER PETE

ROZELL., A N. F. L. WATCH, A N. F. L. BLANKET, AND AN N. F. L.
LAMP.

LOVE IS CATHY HICKS AND HER FAMILY.

LOVE IS THE MEMPHIS PREP FOOTBALL TEAM AND A SPECIAL
AUTOGRAPHED HELMET.

LOVE IS MAXINE PHILLIPS - SEEING TO IT THAT WE ALL
HAD TICKETS TO EACH FRIDAY NIGHT'S GAME.

LOVE IS BOB AND NANCY GOING TO THE GAMES WITH
LILA AND I EACH FRIDAY NIGHT. THE BALDRIDGES - SPECIAL PEOPLE
TO US SINCE OUR TRANSFER TO MEMPHIS. FORGIVING, UNDERSTANDING,
AND GOOD LISTENERS. OUR FIRST THANKSGIVING IN MEMPHIS WE SPENT
WITH BOB, NANCY, JOE AND JENNY.

LOVE IS MARYLYLE AND RODNEY - SEEING TO IT THAT
SCOTT GOT TO THE GAMES ON TIME AND WAS COMFORTABLE THE ENTIRE
NIGHT.

LOVE IS HOUSTON AND LAVERNE - OSCAR AND IMOGENE -
TRAVELING FROM SAND MT., AND CHATTANOOGA TO SEE US. THESE
PEOPLE HAVE ALWAYS BEEN SPECIAL TO ME, SINCE I CAME INTO THE
YOUNG/CHESSER CLAN. THEY ARE SO REAL AND ARE THE SAME EVERY
TIME YOU SEE THEM. GOOD FOLKS - IN FACT, THEY RANK IN THE
SAME CATEGORY AS AUNT BERT AND UNCLE JACK (DADDY'S SISTER AND
BROTHER-IN-LAW, LONG GONE, BUT NOT FORGOTTEN.)

LOVE IS COACH PHILLIPS COMING BY EACH SATURDAY
MORNING, SHOWING THE GAME FILMS - TALKING FOOTBALL TALK.

LOVE IS PRETTY CAROL WOOD AND HER MANY, MANY CARDS,
LETTERS, THOUGHTS, AND PRAYERS. LIKE SUZANNE, SHE IS AS PRETTY
ON THE INSIDE AS SHE IS ON THE OUTSIDE.

LOVE IS A CHRISTIAN S. S. TEACHER - BROOKS LAMMY, WHO CARES.

LOVE IS JENNY BALDRIDGE AND THE RELATIONSHIP OF TRUST AND SHARING THAT HAS DEVELOPED BETWEEN HER AND KELLY.

LOVE IS COL. AND MRS. BOONE - SENDING SCOTT HIS OWN KEY TO THE SPECIAL CHURCH LIFT.

LOVE IS MEMPHIS PREP PEOPLE.

LOVE IS ALL THOSE PEOPLE THAT WERE INVOLVED IN THE PLANNING AND PREPARATION FOR SCOTT'S SPECIAL WEEK.

LOVE IS "SKATE FOR SCOTT."

LOVE IS "THURSDAY NIGHT MOVIE FOR SCOTT."

LOVE IS THE FULL PAGE PICTURE OF SCOTT IN EACH AND EVERY FOOTBALL PROGRAM.

LOVE IS DEDICATING THE ENTIRE FOOTBALL SEASON TO SCOTT.

LOVE IS THE RETIRING OF #89.

LOVE IS SCOTT GOING TO THE CENTER OF THE FIELD WITH LONG TIME FRIENDS, DARRYL AND GARY, FOR THE OFFICIAL COIN TOSS.

LOVE IS JANIE MOREL AND THE SMILE ON HER FACE.

LOVE IS AN ALL NIGHT "SCOTT HOP."

LOVE IS PARENTS, COACHES, TEACHERS, FRIENDS, AND FELLOW STUDENTS IN RED JERSEYS, W/"SCOTT HOP" PRINTED ON THEM.

LOVE IS A JOLLY PERSON SARA PRATHER, LOTS OF FEELING/ LOTS OF FUN.

LOVE IS RON OLSON AND THE OTHER D. J. THAT STAYED ALL NIGHT.

LOVE IS MARLYN AND HER CAMERA.

LOVE IS A SONG,"YOUR ONE IN A MILLION"

LOVE IS DR. DAVIS - PROFESSIONAL, CARING, LOVING.

LOVE IS THE MEMORIES OF A SPECIAL WEEK.

LOVE IS THE SPECIAL BEAUTIFUL PHOTO ALBUMS, CREATED BY MARYLYN - GIVEN IN LOVE.

LOVE IS A SIGNED FOOTBALL FROM THE S. B. E. C. TEAM.

LOVE IS WHITEHAVEN BAPTIST CHURCH.

LOVE IS THE COLLEGE AND CAREER DEPARTMENT.

LOVE IS THE LITTLE LADY THAT KEPT "FINDING THINGS IN PARKING LOTS"!

LOVE IS GENE AND JIMMY TAKING SCOTT TO EAT BARBECUE ON SATURDAY. I CAN'T SAY ENOUGH ABOUT THESE TWO FRIENDS. ALWAYS THERE, SO GENTLE, SO CARING, SO CONCERNED.

LOVE IS BILL SMITH AND THE SMILE ON HIS FACE.

LOVE IS TOTALLY DELIGHTFUL SARA HARBUCK - A TRUE PRODUCT OF SPECIAL PARENTS, CARROLL AND BOBBIE.

LOVE IS LILA'S SUNDAY SCHOOL CLASS - A SPECIAL GROUP OF LADIES.

LOVE IS MY FRIEND, VIRGINIA PENTECOST AND HER HUSBAND MILLER. MRS. P. - WIFE, MOTHER, AND GRANDMOTHER, SUPER SUNDAY SCHOOL TEACHER, REAL WORLD COMMON SENSE, EVERY DAY PERSON - ALL COMBINED WITH MUCH BEAUTY AND LOVE.

LOVE IS CARROLL AND BOBBIE - REAL PEOPLE, WHO HAVE BEEN 'WITH US' EVERY DAY. WE FEEL IT.

LOVE IS A PAIR OF WESTERN BOOTS - ALONG WITH HAT AND JACKET, IN SCOTT'S SIZE - THAT APPEARED AT OUR DOOR ONE SUNDAY AFTERNOON.

LOVE IS TIM WEBB AND JEFF MAXWELL - HELPING IN ANY
WAY - FROM MOVING THE HOSPITAL BED TO CUTTING DOWN AND HAULING
OFF A GOOD SIZE PINE TREE. JEFF AND I OPERATING LIKE TWO BULLS
IN THE MUCH DISCUSSED CHINA SHOP, WHILE TIM, THINKING THE
SITUATION OUT, GETTING US BACK ON TRACK.

LOVE IS THAT GROUP OF MEN - YOUNG AND OLD - WITH
NOTHING TO BE GAINED FINANCIALLY OR EGO-WISE - THAT GAVE OF
THEIR VALUABLE TIME IN HELPING TO ERECT SCOTT'S ROOM.

LOVE IS A MOTHER SUCH AS LILA - WHO CONSTANTLY
GIVES UNSELFISHLY OF HERSELF. THERE ARE MOTHERS AND THEN
THERE ARE SPECIAL MOTHERS. LILA FALLS INTO THAT SPECIAL GROUP!

LOVE IS A DAUGHTER AND SISTER SUCH AS KELLY. SEN-
SITIVE, LOVING, CARING, AND PRETTY ON TOP OF THAT. LOVE IS
THE RELATIONSHIP AND BOND BETWEEN SCOTT AND KELLY.

LOVE IS SCOTT, HIS GRIN, HIS SENSE OF HUMOR, HIS
VERY BEING - HIS PRESENCE IN OUR HOME.

LOVE IS SITTING AROUND THE TABLE AFTER SUPPER -
JUST THE FOUR OF US,JUST FOR A LITTLE WHILE.

LOVE IS NOT A PERSON THAT WOULD TAKE ADVANTAGE -
BUT I'M TOLD THAT WHEN YOU PRAY - GOD DOES NOT HEAR YOUR RE-
QUESTS IF YOU HAVE ANY RESENTMENT OR DISGUST IN YOUR HEART
TOWARD ANY PERSON. I HAVE DEALT WITH MY PROBLEM - GOD UNDER-
STANDS - I'M OKAY NOW!!

LOVE IS DEE CALVERT - A GOOD LOOKING/TOTAL CLASS
INDIVIDUAL.

LOVE IS MRS. LOWREY ,WHO CARES AND HAS MONITORED
SCOTT'S - TO AND FROM - PREP TRANSPORTATION.

LOVE IS THAT FAITHFUL GROUP OF YOUNG MEN THAT HAVE
ASSISTED.

LOVE IS MR. 'MACK', TAKING CARE OF THE ODDS AND ENDS -
MAKING SURE THE MECHANICS ARE WELL OILED AND RUNNING.

LOVE IS GARY HILL - HAS ALWAYS AND WILL ALWAYS BE,
WELCOME IN OUR HOME. A TRUE FRIEND.

GENE, JIMMY, AND GARY - WHAT CAN I SAY? IF THEY
WERE GOING, SCOTT HAS FIT INTO THEIR PLANS. I REALLY CAN'T
SAY ENOUGH ABOUT SCOTT'S FRIENDS - MALE AND FEMALE. WE HEAR
SO MUCH ABOUT THE BAD GUYS AND GALS - IT SELLS NEWSPAPERS.
I WISH THAT I COULD PRINT MY OWN BRAND OF PAPER ABOUT PREP
PEOPLE.

LOVE IS KIRK MILNER, COMING BY TO SHOW SOME "EARLY
JOCK" FOOTBALL FILMS.

LOVE IS FRANK THOMAS - SEEING TO IT THAT SCOTT
(ALL OF US) HAD FRESH CRAPPIE FILETS ON A REGULAR BASIS.

LOVE IS ONE OF BEAR BRYANT'S FORMER STUDENTS -
JACK DAY - CARING, TOUCHING BASES, HELPING, AND FINDING WAYS
TO CUT THE RED TAPE.

LOVE IS TAYLOR'S MOTHER - MRS. 'C' - SENDING CANDY
IN ENVELOPES TO SCOTT.

LOVE IS FRANK THOMAS, A MAN'S MAN, AND A TRUE
FRIEND, TAKING THE TIME - AND WHO CAN PUT A PRICE ON TIME,
TO TRANSPORT SCOTT DOWN TO HIS HUNTING CAMP AT TUNICA. TRULY
ONE OF SCOTT'S MOST ENJOYABLE DAYS! "DAD, I'D LIKE TO SPEND
THE WHOLE DAY DOWN HERE." "WHAT WOULD YOU DO, SCOTT?" JUST
SIT HERE AND ENJOY IT."

AND SO IT GOES, ON AND ON! LOVE BEING EXPRESSED
IN SO MANY, MANY WONDERFUL WAYS. IN THIS LITTLE RAMBLING NOTE,
I HAVE TOUCHED ONLY THE TIP OF THE ICEBERG SO TO SPEAK. * I
KNOW THAT I HAVE LEFT OUT PERSONALITIES, SITUATIONS, AND EVENTS.
PEOPLE THAT HAVE LOVED AND CARED. GOD HAS TRULY BLESSED
BILL COLEMAN'S FAMILY.

BUT YOU KNOW, THESE SPECIAL PEOPLE WEREN'T ACTING
SPECIAL - THEY WERE JUST BEING THEMSELVES."

DEAR GOD - I ASK YOUR FORGIVENESS FOR WHEN I HAVE
FAILED YOU AND HAVE DISAPPOINTED YOU. I KNOW IN MY HEART THAT
I HAVE DONE MANY THINGS TO HURT YOU. GOD, I THANK YOU FOR THE
GOOD TIMES AND THE BAD TIMES, FOR THE PEAKS AND THE VALLEYS,
FOR FRIENDS AND LOVE ONES, FOR PEOPLE I HAVE PREVIOUSLY TAKEN
FOR GRANTED. I THANK YOU FOR STRENGTH, COURAGE, AND WISDOM THAT
ONLY YOU CAN GIVE. YOU HAVE BEEN SO GOOD TO MY FAMILY. I
THANK YOU FOR KEEPING SCOTT'S LUNGS CLEAR. I THANK YOU FOR A
MOTHER SUCH AS LILA AND FOR A DAUGHTER AND SISTER SUCH AS KELLY.
I THANK YOU FOR THE PROMISES YOU HAVE GIVEN US. IN JESUS NAME
I LIFT SCOTT UP TO YOU AND ASK FOR THE COMPLETE HEALING OF HIS
BODY. MAKE US WORTHY. IN JESUS NAME I PRAY.

AMEN

FOLKS - THANKS FOR SHOWING ME THE REAL MEANING OF
LOVE.

Bill

BILL

PICTURES FROM TODAY

Aubrey. One more precious reason I wrote this book.

Linda's Parents Celebrate 50 Years of Marriage

More of my best! Coleman, Abby, Zach, and Lexus.

My friend Lindsay! Lindsay and her husband Aaron, both
have full-time jobs, two wonderful children and a tremendous
amount of extracurricular activities. Lindsay has also begun a
second career as a photographer. Somehow they found time
to not only spend a couple of days taking pictures for the
cover, but also volunteer to read, help me correct and clarify
a tremendous amount of this book. Incredible friends and
incredible encouragement! The Keegan's taught me a lesson about
friendship. At times, making a friend's priority your priority
is the best way to express how important you are to them.

Taylor, Marcus, and Scott at Como Steakhouse.

The Best Part of the Cabin...sharing it
with friends like the Brookleres

Coleman and Zach with Me watching the Tigers on
their way to a national championship! War Eagle!

CPSIA information can be obtained at www.ICGtesting.com
Printed in the USA
LVOW041617031112

305598LV00003B/5/P